AMERICA'S
· GREAT ·
DISASTERS

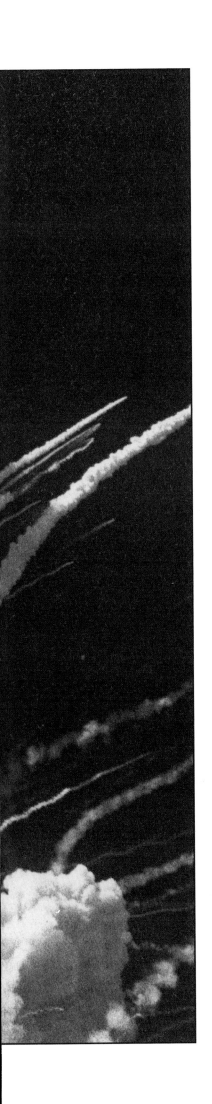

AMERICA'S
· GREAT ·
DISASTERS

Candace Floyd

MALLARD
PRESS

Text
Candace Floyd

Photography
United Press International/Bettmann

Design
Jill Coote

Commissioning Editor
Andrew Preston

Publishing Assistant
Edward Doling

Photo Research
Leora Kahn

Editor
Jane Adams

Production
Ruth Arthur
David Proffit
Sally Connolly

Director of Production
Gerald Hughes

Director of Publishing
David Gibbon

MALLARD PRESS

An imprint of BDD Promotional Books Company, Inc,
666 Fifth Avenue, New York, N.Y. 10103.

Mallard Press and its accompanying design and logo
are trademarks of BDD Promotional Book Company, Inc.

CLB 2348
© 1990 Archive Publishing, a division of Colour Library Books Ltd,
Godalming, Surrey, England.
First published in the United States of America
in 1990 by The Mallard Press.
Printed and bound in Italy by New Interlitho.
All rights reserved.
ISBN 0 792 45381 6

CONTENTS

INTRODUCTION

WHEN DISASTER STRIKES

The history of America is filled with stories of disasters. Whether man-made, like the Great Chicago Fire of 1871, or natural, like the eruption of Mount St. Helens in 1981 and the 1964 Alaska earthquake, disasters bring out special qualities in the survivors.

In the pages of *America's Great Disasters* are stories of bravery and stamina, and of a great determination to help the unfortunate victims.

Few modern-day city managers can match the speed and efficiency of Mayor Walter C. Jones in Galveston when he surveyed his devastated island city and took immediate steps to organize relief. Few city dwellers can match the perseverance of the residents of Centralia, Pennsylvania, who struggled for twenty-three years to keep their lives intact as a mine fire raged out of control deep beneath their homes.

America's Great Disasters relates the story of American munificence. Whenever disaster strikes, Americans reach deep into their pockets to donate money to relief efforts, or they race to the scene to help victims rebuild. When Galveston was destroyed by a hurricane in 1900, the residents of Johnstown, Pennsylvania, who were still struggling to recover from a devastating flood in their valley in 1889, nevertheless raised money for Galveston. When Hurricane Hugo struck South Carolina, hundreds of volunteers sped to the area to help survivors rebuild their homes and businesses.

The American Red Cross, founded in 1881 by Clara Barton, continues to organize relief operations to this day. In 1882, the Red Cross doled out aid to victims of the Mississippi River and Ohio River floods. In 1884, survivors of another flood of the Ohio River received food, clothing, blankets, and fuel from Red Cross volunteers. When an epidemic of yellow fever broke out in Jascksonville, Florida, trained Red Cross nurses moved to the town to care for the sick. In 1893, a hurricane swept over Sea Islands near the coast of South Carolina, and Red Cross volunteers helped the residents rebuild their lives. Clara Barton stayed in Johnstown and in Galveston for months after the disasters there. In Galveston, she organized a new orphanage and set up soup kitchens to feed the city's hungry residents. After Barton's death in 1912, the Red Cross provided aid to thousands of disaster victims, including those of 1989's Hurricane Hugo and San Francisco earthquake.

RIGHT: The remains of a residential area in Gainesville, Georgia, on April 7, 1936, the day after a tremendous tornado swept through the southern United States. More than 400 people were killed and a further 2,000 were injured by the tornado, which touched down in Georgia, Alabama, Mississippi, Tennessee, and Arkansas.

America's Great Disasters also relates the stories of the people held to be at fault. In Johnstown, residents filed damage suits against the South Fork Hunting and Fishing Club, owner of the South Fork Dam that had collapsed. Even though the members of the club owned enormous personal assets, the residents of Johnstown received no monetary compensation for their losses. The families of the people who died when the Hyatt Regency's skybridges collapsed received twenty-nine million dollars in out-of-court settlements from the hotel and the architects, engineers, and contractors involved in the design and construction of the building.

America's Great Disasters presents the stories of both the people who died and the people who survived, from the Chicago Fire in 1871 to the San Francisco earthquake in 1989.

CHAPTER ONE
FLOODS AND DAM FAILURES

Nearly every school-age child knows the story of Noah's Ark. According to the Biblical account, God decided to destroy the earth, because it had become wicked and corrupt in the 1,600 years after the creation of Adam. Only one man, Noah, and his family would be saved. God instructed Noah to build an ark and to gather a male and a female of every living species within its sturdy walls. For forty days and forty nights, the rain sent by God to purge the earth of wickedness continued to fall. When the rain stopped and the waters receded, Noah's ark was resting on the mountain of Ararat.

Archaeologists and other scholars have searched for traces of the ark on Mount Ararat in Turkey for years but have found no physical evidence that it ever existed. Whether the story is based on an actual global flood or is simply an amalgamation of stories of several ancient floods in the Mesopotamian region, Noah's flood and others since have brought new beginnings for those who survived.

LEFT: A gaping hole at the corner of the Teton Dam, where water rushed through on June 5, 1976, to cover several small towns in the area, causing damage totaling more than $500 million.

RIGHT: One of the most popular views for photographers after the 1889 flood in Johnstown was a house at Main and Union streets, where the raging water had driven an uprooted tree through the wrecked home.

THE JOHNSTOWN FLOOD 1889

As many as 500 people died in the Mississippi River flood of 1927. When the dam broke in Buffalo Hollow, 118 people perished; sixty-nine Austin residents died in the flood of 1911. Dayton, Ohio, flooded in the spring of 1913, when the Ohio River roared out of its banks and swept between 500 and 700 people to their deaths. Rapid City, South Dakota, disappeared underwater when Canyon Lake Dam burst, killing 200 people. However, the worst flood in the United States' history was in 1889 in Johnstown, Pennsylvania. Here, in a matter of hours, 2,209 people met their deaths.

The flood was caused by the collapse of the dam holding Lake Conemaugh, high in the Allegheny Mountains above Johnstown. Seventy-two feet high and more than 900 feet long, the South Fork Dam, as Johnstown residents called it, was made of earth. Streams and creeks in that section of the Alleghenies fed the lake, which held some twenty million tons of water, at full capacity.

The dam was originally built by the state of Pennsylvania to solve the summer water shortages that plagued the Western Division Railroad's Portage Road. The dam consisted of layers of clay, coated with loose rocks on both its inner and outer faces. A seventy-two-foot-wide spillway was cut at the eastern side of the dam. In width, the dam measured twenty feet at the top and 270 feet at the base. At the center of the dam, five cast-iron pipes were set in place to release water down the Little Conemaugh River whenever the level of the lake rose too high.

The Pennsylvania Railroad bought the property in 1857, and for years no maintenance was done on the dam. In 1862, the dam failed but, because a vigilant watchman had released much of the water as soon as he suspected trouble, no damage occurred below in the valley. The lake remained, much diminished in size, until first a Pennsylvania congressman bought the property in 1875, and then Benjamin F. Ruff, as a representative of the South Fork Fishing and Hunting Club, purchased it in 1879. Before the congressman sold the dam and surrounding property to Ruff, he removed the discharge pipes, figuring he could make a little money by selling them for scrap. Ruff repaired the dam after a fashion. He added steel pipes to form a screen at the spillway, thus keeping the club's freshly stocked fish from swimming downstream. He also dumped rocks, mud, brush, hay, and all kinds of other materials around the base of the dam, but he did not replace the discharge pipes.

RIGHT: On May 30, 1889, an earthen dam at South Fork Lake in the Allegheny Mountains of Pennsylvania collapsed, spilling 20 million tons of water onto the valley below. In Johnstown and several other towns and villages in the valley, 2,209 people died as the water splintered their homes and businesses and carried them downstream.

LEFT: The Cambria Iron Works after the Johnstown flood.

ABOVE: A young victim of the Johnstown flood.

The South Fork Fishing and Hunting Club owned not only the dam, but also about 160 acres that surrounded it. On this land, the members erected a clubhouse, cottages that were individually owned, boathouses, and stables. Among the early members of the club were several wealthy Pittsburgh entrepreneurs including Andrew Carnegie, a Scottish-born industrialist and leader of the American steel industry; Henry Clay Frick, a partner of Carnegie's in the steel industry and later the chairman of Carnegie Steel Company; and Andrew Mellon, an organizer of Gulf Oil and financial backer of the Aluminum Company of America. By 1889, the club membership totaled sixty-one.

While the club was busy repairing the dam, Johnstown citizens grew alarmed. Daniel Johnson Morrell, the manager of the Cambria Iron Works, sent an engineer to inspect the work being done on the dam. The engineer's report cited weaknesses in the structure, including the fact that there were no discharge valves in place. Morrell offered to help the club finance the necessary improvements, but to no avail. The club opted to spend only 17,000 dollars on repairs.

On Friday, May 30, it rained long and hard throughout the area. Johnstown residents feared they would be hit by yet another flood, for the streets of Johnstown were covered each spring when the river crossed its banks. By the afternoon of the next day, water ranging from two feet deep in some places to ten feet deep in others covered the town.

Around noon, the telegraph operator in East Conemaugh, upstream from Johnstown, received a wire that warned of a possible dam break. He sent the message on down the line to Johnstown, where freight agent Frank Dekert spread the word to a few people nearby.

Back at the dam, the club's engineer, John Parke, noted that the water in the lake was rising at the alarming rate of about an inch every ten minutes. Despite the efforts of the men who were piling up earth at the center of the dam and of others who were trying to clear debris from the fish screen at the spillway, Parke realized that the water would soon crest the top. More messages were sent downstream to the community of South Fork and beyond.

Shortly after noon, water began pouring over the top of the dam. The center of the dam soon collapsed, and the full fury of twenty million tons of water was loosed into the valley below. The entire lake emptied in three quarters of an hour at most, and experts later estimated that the force was comparable to that of the water flowing over Niagara Falls.

At South Fork, the water swept into the community in a forty-foot-high-wall. Here, an English coal miner named Michael Mann was the first of many people to die in the flood. In all, three South Fork residents were killed. Also swept away were the planing mill, a bridge, and about twenty other buildings.

Crushing a seventy-five-foot-tall viaduct in its path, the wall of water swept into Mineral Point, a community of some 200 people. Many of the residents had already left for higher ground that morning and early afternoon, but those who remained scrambled quickly onto rooftops or onto the hillside itself. At Mineral Point, the death toll rose to sixteen.

Racing at forty miles an hour down the straightaways, but slowing up a bit in the curvier sections of the valley, the water then poured into East Conemaugh. Some passengers sitting on trains that had been delayed in town because of rain were swept to their deaths; others escaped in the nick of time to high ground. Large buildings, such as the Eagle Hotel, the Central Hotel, the post office, the railroad station, and several stores, as well as thirty locomotives were felled by the wall of water. Added to the debris being swept along by the flood were 200,000 pounds of barbed wire picked up in East Conemaugh.

The flood gathered speed in the straightaway between East Conemaugh and Woodvale, a town built by the Cambria Iron Company and home to 1,000 people. In five brief minutes, the flood washed everything away, leaving behind only a part of the woolen mill and a few houses at the edge of the water's path. One in every three Woodvale residents was killed, making a total of 314.

At 4.07 p.m., a thirty-six-foot wall of water hit Johnstown, which had a population of 10,000 people. In ten minutes, the library, the telegraph office, the opera house, the stone YMCA hall, the German Lutheran church, the fire station, and hundreds of houses were swept before the wall of water. Then the wall crashed against the hill at Stony Creek, creating a huge

LEFT: The huge stone bridge below Johnstown became a dam, blocking the water and debris that had rushed through the valley. Trapped in the debris were 500 to 600 people; all but eighty managed to clamber out of the pile of debris, which caught fire at nightfall.

ABOVE: A view of Clinton and Locust streets, Johnstown, after the flood.

backwash that destroyed many more buildings. People perched on roofs or other parts of buildings were spun madly along the water's course, toward the stone bridge just north of the point where the Little Conemaugh runs into Stony Creek and the Conemaugh River. Protected to some degree by Prospect Hill from the full onslaught of the water, the bridge did not collapse. Instead, with all the debris that was rapidly collecting under its arches, the bridge became a dam, and water backed up all over Johnstown.

As well as boxcars, houses, barbed wire, telegraph poles, and rubbish, the bridge trapped 500 to 600 people, each holding on to whatever they could to stay above the whirling water. Most of these victims managed to claw their way to safety; at least eighty did not. The horror they then endured was beyond belief as night fell and fires broke out in the tangled mess of oil tankers and overturned stoves.

Back in the town, many people spent the night in trees, with twenty-foot-deep water whirling below them.

LEFT: Trains parked along the tracks in East Conemaugh, a few miles south of the South Fork Dam, were tossed about like toys when the water from the lake swept over them.

BELOW: Temporary morgues, such as this one on the banks of the Conemaugh River, were set up in response to a most pressing need after the Johnstown flood.

ABOVE: A view of a house at Main and Union streets, Johnstown, which had been pierced by an uprooted tree.

identify them. Because of their ghastly condition, one out of every three bodies could not be identified, giving a total of 663 unknown dead. The total count of 2,209 dead meant that one out of every ten people living in the valley had died in the flood.

As word spread to Pittsburgh and other cities, contributions totaling more than two and a half million dollars poured into the town, together with trainload after trainload of supplies and food. Clara Barton and volunteers from the Red Cross arrived to provide whatever relief they could. In Johnstown, 7,000 workmen spent three months clearing the debris and burying bodies.

Bodies of flood victims were also washed downstream into the Allegheny River. A day and a half after the flood hit Johnstown, workers in Pittsburgh, seventy-five miles away, pulled the floor of a destroyed home to the shore. To their surprise they found a five-month-old baby who had survived all alone on the floating debris.

Within a matter of days, newspaper headlines screamed that the cause of the flood was the faulty repairs carried out on the dam by the South Fork Fishing and Hunting Club. At coroner's hearings, the club was held responsible time after time, and survivors were soon making claims for damages against the club. To the dismay of the townspeople, the club itself had few resources, despite the personal wealth of its members. As cases went before juries, the club was held to be free of blame, and no one in the valley received any compensation from either the club or its members.

Others crowded into the attics of the few remaining buildings. At sunrise survivors looked around the scene of horror that had once been their town and saw that about 3,000 people had camped for the night on Green Hill. Other hills surrounding the town held similarly sized crowds. All were wet, cold, inadequately clothed, and hungry. Many were gravely injured.

On the afternoon of Sunday, June 1, the townspeople gathered at a meeting in the Adams Street schoolhouse. There they chose Arthur J. Moxman to lead the relief effort. Moxham created committees to perform the most pressing chores of clearing away dead animals, looking for dead people, and setting up morgues and temporary hospitals.

At the morgues, volunteers numbered the bodies as they were brought in and tried as best they could to

LEFT: Huge boulders lying along the shores of East Conemaugh River were lifted by the floodwaters, as they rushed towards Johnstown with a force comparable to the water flowing over Niagara Falls.

BELOW: Some survivors realized a profit from the Johnstown flood, selling souvenirs to a curious public.

ABOVE: The day after the Johnstown flood, survivors found a scene of horror all around them. Bodies lay everywhere.

RIGHT: An 1890 lithograph of the Johnstown flood. As word spread about the disaster, relief workers flocked to the area, and all over the country people donated money to a disaster fund.

MISSISSIPPI RIVER
1927

Over hundreds, perhaps even thousands, of years people living along the banks of the Mississippi have adapted to the river's changing course. Spring brought floods to the land bordering the Father of Waters, and early residents of the area retreated from the banks only to return when the water receded, leaving behind a new layer of extremely fertile soil. By the 1700s, white settlers made a new discovery. If they built earthen dikes along the banks, they could keep the river from spilling over onto their own lands, and force it to flood south of their fields of crops. In the nineteenth century, the river was edged with dikes from Cairo, Illinois, to the Gulf of Mexico – a thousand-mile-long snake of man-made banks.

Despite man's efforts to control the raging waters by building ever higher and thicker dikes, the floods still came. The years 1858, 1862, 1867, 1884, 1890, 1897, 1903, 1912, 1913, and 1922 all saw the Mississippi River run wildly awry from its usual course.

The year 1927 was different only because of the size of the flood that covered the river valley. All through winter and spring, heavy rains plagued the area, and the river's mammoth system of tributaries fed it more water than it could handle. The river valley itself had undergone changes during the nineteenth and early twentieth centuries, and these also contributed to the size of the flood. Loggers and farmers had felled many of the natural forests, that had slowed the course of the flooding river for centuries. Now the waters surged through a riverbed that was lined with dikes that allowed no spillway, no release of pressure.

RIGHT: A bridge barely spans the flood-stage river in St. Louis, Missouri, in April 1927, when the Mississippi River measured a hundred miles wide at some points. Some of the bridges over the river provided a place of refuge for people trying to escape the high water, but once they reached a nearby bridge, they were often stranded for anything from several hours to a few days before rescue boats arrived.

BELOW: At Junior Plantation, forty miles south of New Orleans, Louisiana, the steamship *Inspector* rammed into the levee on April 27, 1927. Captain Casey ordered his crew to position the ship in such a way as to block the flooding water from rushing through the crevasse. Nevertheless, more than 15,000 acres were flooded as a result of the break.

Residents of the Mississippi River valley worried about those dikes they had built. Were they strong enough to hold the waters? Were they high enough? Over the years the Mississippi River Commission, a Congressionally appointed agency, had adopted a policy of "dikes only" for controlling floods. The agency, along with the Army Corps of Engineers, had set a standard height for the dikes they built, a standard based on the highest previous water level.

On April 21, 1927, the Mississippi River Commission's standard proved insufficient. At Mound Landing, Mississippi, and at Pendleton, Arkansas, the river broke through the levees and poured unchecked through the area. The break on the Mississippi side alone flooded more than two million acres and caused 172,770 people to flee their homes. The next break, at Cabin Teele, Louisiana, flooded more than six million acres.

The crevasse, or break, at Mound Landing was only one of 120 dike failures that terrified valley residents that spring. At the moment of the break, workers were piling sandbags on top of the levee, trying desperately to raise its height and keep the water from spilling over. When the break occurred, many of the workers fell into the water and were swept away, although no one knows the exact number.

As word about the crevasse spread, residents fled to the only high ground around – the levee itself. There they stayed until rescue boats arrived to take them to refugee camps. In Helena, Arkansas, 2,000 people struggled to stay above the water on the dikes at Knowlton's Landing. Screaming for help as the dikes crumbled under their feet, they summoned the steamer Wabash to their aid.

The water spread slowly across the land. Beyond the break itself, where witnesses likened the noise to that of a wild animal's roar, the water did not rage. Instead, it seeped into ever wider areas at the rate of about fourteen miles a day. Soon the river itself measured 100 miles wide in some areas.

The day after the Mound Landing crevasse, the residents of Greenville, Mississippi, learned that the protective dikes surrounding their city were not sufficient to steer the flood away from their homes. Water poured into the town, and people scattered to the second stories of buildings or to unbroken sections of the levee. As the levees bordering the Arkansas River gave way at dozens of different points, about 500 people ran to the Free Bridge, which spanned the river with steel. There they remained for several days, unable to leave because the bridge access ramps on both sides of the river were under water. Other Arkansan refugees fled to Pine Bluff, where life remained almost normal despite the water covering the lower sections of the town. At specific locations throughout the city, people caught boats the way New Yorkers catch taxi cabs, to make the trip to the store for supplies. A correspondent reported in the April 26 issue of *The New York Times* that

from his vantage point on the bluffs of Memphis, Tennessee, the only things visible across the river in Arkansas were the tops of trees.

New Orleans' residents watched anxiously as dikes to the north broke and the water level at the city's levee rose higher each day. City leaders devised a plan to save New Orleans from the flood. They decided to break through the levee south of the city at Caernarvon and to take responsibility for the people living in the parishes of Plaquemines and St. Bernard, as they would be affected by the flood that would inevitably follow. On May 3, a diver set off dynamite charges under the levee at Caernarvon, and the water swept across the two parishes.

LEFT: Wherever the water was waist high, automobiles became useless as modes of transportation. Mississippi farm families relied on their horses and wagons for travel. More than 600,000 people throughout the river valley were left homeless.

BELOW: The flooding water of the Mississippi River smashed everything in its path. This train trestle in Yazoo, Mississippi, experienced the full fury of the April 1927 flood.

James Fieser of the Red Cross and Herbert Hoover, secretary of commerce under President Calvin Coolidge, brought their agencies to the aid of flood refugees. Vicksburg was the headquarters of the Red Cross's relief work. In Mississippi, Arkansas, and Louisiana, the three states most heavily damaged by the flood, the Red Cross provided food and shelter for more than 300,000 people. The organization established 154 refugee camps all along the valley. Four were located at the national park in Vicksburg. The Red Cross raised fifteen million dollars in relief funds, the Rockefeller Foundation provided one million dollars for a sanitation fund, and the U.S. Chamber of Commerce set aside ten million dollars to provide low-interest loans to the residents of the stricken area.

The predominantly rural folks who made their way to the Red Cross camps found a new way of life there. These independent farm families were forced into a regimen alien to their nature, though necessary for order. After leaving the boats that brought them to the camps, refugees registered at the site. Accustomed to hard work from sunrise to sunset, they now had idle hours on their hands. Demonstration workers set out to fill some of those hours, leading classes on rug making, quilting, sewing, mattress making, and furniture refinishing, which were all skills that would come in handy once the refugees returned to their drenched homes.

LEFT: Greenville, Mississippi, and dozens of other towns in the Mississippi River Valley were washed away when the river broke through the levees along its shore in the spring of 1927. When this photograph was taken, 12,000 of Greenville's 15,000 residents had been evacuated from their homes. For years, the Mississippi River Commission, a Congressionally appointed agency, had been insisting that the dikes and levees were adequate protection for the valuable farmlands and growing cities along the river.

The camps were not without scandals. Black leaders discovered that peonage was rampant in the camps, and they demanded that Herbert Hoover establish a Colored Advisory Commission to root out any trace of debt servitude. The problem arose because, once in the camps, refugees were not allowed to leave unless they were sponsored by an outside person who promised to care for them. Planters in the area kept these outside people, labor agents from the north, from entering the camps, so that, when the time came for the refugees to leave, they did so under the sponsorship of the planters who leased land to them for tenant farming.

Another scandal was the spread of venereal disease. After months of ignoring the problem, Red Cross officials brought in volunteers from the American School Hygiene Association of New York who gave lectures on hygiene and the dangers of promiscuity.

As the flood waters receded, refugees began to think of their return home. What they imagined was unbearable. Had their homes been swept away? Had their barns and other outbuildings been washed down to the Gulf of Mexico? Had their livestock, which they had carefully shut away in barn lofts, survived? Again the

Red Cross came to their aid, supplying furniture, food, clothing, feed for animals, farm tools, and seed. On his side, Hoover met with town leaders to set up credit organizations for flood victims.

In the seven states affected by the flood, more than sixteen million acres of land were covered by the waters. By the end of the flood, farmers had totaled up losses of 102 million dollars in crops. In all, more than 600,000 people were evacuated from the area. Their livestock bore the brunt of the disaster – one million chickens, 9,000 work animals, 26,000 head of cattle, and 127,000 hogs were lost. No one knows how many people died in the flood of 1927, but estimates range from 250 to 500.

ABOVE: The American Red Cross established tented refugee camps, such as this one in Hickman, Kentucky, along the Mississippi River Valley. It was an alien way of life for most of the homeless farm families. To fill the idle hours, demonstration workers taught skills the refugees would need when they returned to their flood-damaged homes.

LEFT: If a crevasse occurred in a levee along the Mississippi River, people would head for high ground, most often the levee itself. Residents of Greenville, Mississippi, flocked to the levee with their horses and cattle in April 1927. As their town disappeared under water, they waited there for rescue boats to take them to the Red Cross refugee camps.

BUFFALO HOLLOW, WEST VIRGINIA 1972

The Appalachian Mountains are dotted with mining camps. Rich with coal deposits, the mountainsides provide work for thousands of people, who daily make the trek from their homes to strip mines or mine shafts.

In 1972, however, the mountains brought death and destruction to residents of Buffalo Hollow in Logan County, West Virginia.

During World War II, the Lorado Coal Mining Company began to strip mine the coal deposits from the sides of the mountains in Buffalo Hollow. Slag – the slate and other rock covering the coal – was dumped by the company's workers into a narrow valley near the head of the hollow. Over the years, the pile of slag dammed up the hollow's tributary system, creating a long lake behind the dump. After the war, the Buffalo Mining Company bought the mines and continued to strip mine the area. As more and more strip mining caused rainfall to flow directly into the lake and as water was pumped from mine shafts at the rate of 360,000 gallons a year, one lake became three, all of which were filled with acidic, black water.

On the morning of February 26, 1972, water in the largest of the lakes was only a foot or so from the top of the slag pile. Deputy Sheriff Otto Mutters heard reports of the dangerously high water level and went to the site to inspect it himself. Convinced that disaster was imminent, he set out to warn valley residents. Early that morning, mine employees were also spreading the word, but few residents took heed.

At a few minutes after 8.00 a.m., the slag-pile dam gave way, and twenty million cubic feet of water unleashed its power on the valley. The small village of Saunders was hit first. Houses and churches were swept before the flood. The next village, Pardee, had no defense against the forty-foot-high wall of black water. In the next town down the valley, Lorado, the water smashed the homes of 500 residents and tore railroad tracks from their ties. Lundale, Stowe, and Crites were next. Midway down the hollow at Amhersdale, the water spread out to 500 yards across but was still twenty feet high. By the time the water reached Man at the mouth of the hollow, the force had abated, but it still carried tons of mud along with it into homes and businesses.

The first report of damage announced that 1,500 people were missing. The United States Army, the Salvation Army, and the Red Cross poured into the valley immediately. They flew in food and water purification systems, set up mobile kitchens, and provided mobile homes for the victims. Days would pass before the death toll became final – 114 known dead, four unknown dead, and twenty people missing.

Who was at fault? The Buffalo Mining Company disclaimed responsibility for the flood. Company officials said that the state of West Virginia had not allowed the company to release water from the lakes to relieve pressure on the slag pile. State officials could find no record of such a request, although a review of the state's records did show that state inspectors had not examined the dam for more than a year before the break.

On September 6, the investigating committee appointed by Governor A.A. Moore, Jr., charged that the Pittston Company, which owned the Buffalo Mining Company, had showed "flagrant disregard" for the residents of the hollow. Over the following weeks, more than 650 flood victims filed suit against the Buffalo Mining Company and the Pittston Company for sixty-four million dollars in damages. On July 5, 1974, the Pittston Company settled the damage suit out of court for thirteen and a half million dollars. Each plaintiff received an average of 20,640 dollars.

ABOVE: The dam at the head of Buffalo Hollow two days after it burst, allowing tons of water to ravage the entire valley. Before the break, several houses had been located in the foreground. These houses, and hundreds of others, were swept away in the flood. The dam was made of spoil – scrap slate and other rock taken from mining shafts. Over the years, the dam backed up both streams and water pumped out of the Buffalo Mining Company's shafts, forming three lakes of black, acidic water.

LEFT: A highway lined with debris, the day after the flood in Buffalo Valley. Immediately after the flood, the U.S. Army, the Salvation Army, and the American Red Cross rushed to the area to provide aid to victims.

RIGHT: The steel bridge at the left of this photograph was originally located approximately where the dump truck is parked in the background. When the dam in Buffalo Hollow collapsed, the bridge was swept off its foundations. During the weeks after the flood, more than 650 people filed suits against the Pittston Company, owner of the Buffalo Mining Company and its dam. The plaintiffs received average payments of $20,640 in out-of-court settlements.

ABOVE: Piles of rubbish left behind by the Buffalo Hollow flood in Bacco. Following the collapse of the 200-foot-high dam on February 26, 1972, nearly twenty million cubic feet of water rushed through the valley, wiping out fourteen towns and killing 118 people.

LEFT: A house in the Santa Clara River Valley that was swept several feet downstream from its original location by raging floodwaters after the collapse of the St. Francis Dam.

BELOW: Approximately twelve billion gallons of water were stored in the reservoir behind the St. Francis Dam near Los Angeles. When the dam collapsed on March 13, 1928, all the bridges in the Santa Clara valley were swept away by the water, rushing at 500,000 cubic feet per second.

RIGHT: More than 350 people drowned in the flood caused by the St. Francis Dam collapse. Immediately after the break, 700 people were reported missing. This aerial photograph shows the devastated area near Santa Paula, California.

LEFT: Victims of the flood caused by the collapse of the St. Francis Dam gather in Santa Paula to collect the supplies they need to rebuild their lives. Hundreds of people were left homeless after the disaster.

BELOW: Throughout the valley below the St. Francis Dam, whole towns and villages were laid to waste. A layer of thick silt covered ranch lands after the water receded.

FAR LEFT: Rescue workers carrying the dead out of the area devastated by the St. Francis Dam collapse and flood. More than 2,000 rescue workers searched the area. Whenever they found a body, they placed a scrap of cloth on a stick pushed into the ground. As work progressed, hundreds of white flag markers waved in the breeze.

ABOVE: Maneuvering in the streets of Pittsburgh after the Monongahela River flooded in March 1936 was best done in boats. Cities and towns throughout the northeast – including Deerfield, Massachusetts;

Binghamton, New York; Hartford, Connecticut; and Hatfield, Massachusetts – were plagued by floods in the spring of 1936, when heavy rains overflowed the banks of rivers.

TOP RIGHT: One policeman patrols the streets of Pittsburgh after the March 1936 flood, while another carries a man caught in the swirling waters.

RIGHT: Half-submerged trolley cars in the downtown section. The March 1936 flood in Pittsburgh caused damage totaling millions of dollars.

LEFT: An aerial view of Pittsburgh where flood waters invaded homes and businesses and smoke from the Waverly Oil Company fire filled the skies in March 1936. Business came to a complete, if temporary, halt in the city.

TOP LEFT: Fire broke out at the Waverly Oil Company in Pittsburgh on March 18, 1936, and swept through the plant, which covered a two-block-long area, adding to the horror of the flood.

ABOVE: "Smoke City," as Pittsburgh was sometimes called, proved worthy of its name as the Waverly Oil Company fire raged in March 1936.

LEFT: In Youngstown, Ohio, people crowd into a wagon, pulled by mules, to make their way through the city during the January 1937 flood.

BELOW: The flooding Ohio River caused property damage totaling $418 million in January 1937. Towns affected by rising waters in the Ohio and Mississippi river valleys that month included Pittsburgh and Johnstown, Pennsylvania; Cincinnati, Ohio; Evansville, Indiana; Aurora and Cairo, Illinois; Louisville, Kentucky.

ABOVE When the Ohio River poured over its banks in January 1937, people in Marietta, Ohio, used small boats to travel around the city.

RIGHT: An aerial view of Manhattan, Kansas, after the Kansas River flooded in July 1951.

BELOW: President Truman flies over Kansas City to view the damage caused in the area when theKansas River flooded in July 1951.

LEFT: In March 1973, winds and rain aggravated an already high Lake Ontario and forced the evacuation of many homes along the lake's shore. Sandbags were used to build walls in an attempt to prevent the water eroding house foundations in Rochester, New York.

BELOW: All hands and all means were used to fill sandbags to hold back the angry waters of Lake Ontario in March 1973.

ABOVE: On June 5, 1976, the Teton Dam near Idaho Falls, Idaho, collapsed and six towns in the Snake River Valley were flooded by water moving at the rate of fifteen miles an hour. In

September 1976, President Gerald Ford signed a bill that provided for compensation to the victims of the Teton Dam collapse.

RIGHT: An aerial view showing the gaping hole in the Teton Dam, Idaho, through which a wall of water poured in June 1976.

RIGHT: An aerial view of the scene in Rexburg, Idaho, on June 5, 1976, the day of the Teton Dam collapse. A total of about 30,000 people were evacuated from the region.

BELOW: A wall of water fifteen feet high swept through Rexburg, Idaho, after the Teton Dam collapse. Eight people were killed and fires broke out throughout Rexburg, the town hardest hit by the flood, as gas lines were snapped in two by the floodwaters.

CHAPTER TWO

DROUGHT

The following scene is familiar to everyone who has read John Steinbeck's *The Grapes of Wrath*: poor, hungry farm families traveling in broken-down cars loaded with their few paltry belongings. Millions of people left the Great Plains during the 1930s, traveling to California and the Pacific Northwest where they hoped to find a better life. Propelling them from their homes and farms was not only the economic depression, but also the great dust storms and crop failures they suffered during the worst drought in American history. The world's breadbasket had turned, seemingly overnight, into the Dust Bowl.

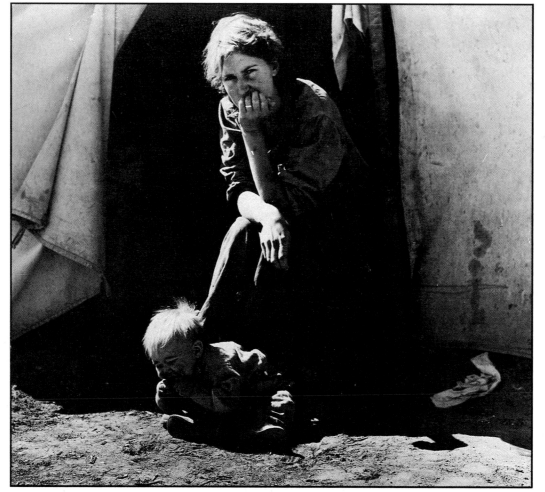

LEFT: Poverty and despair plagued the lives of farmers and their families during the 1930s drought, as can be seen from this ca. 1934 photograph of a sharecropper's wife and child.

RIGHT: The Great American Dust Bowl. This photograph by Rothstein shows conditions in 1933 in the western states. In a matter of a few years, the nation's bread basket turned into a desert.

THE DUST BOWL
1930s

In the spring of 1930, the seasonal rains that farmers depended on for nourishing their newly planted seedlings did not come. Not only was rainfall below normal in the Midwest, it also fell far short of the norm in the East, from Maryland and Virginia to Missouri and Arkansas. However, from 1931, it was the Great Plains that bore the brunt of the drought. Over the next few years temperatures well over 100°F accompanied the drought, and people throughout the region died from the excessive heat.

Strong westerly winds boiled up black clouds of churning dust that swept across the region. Day turned to night as the thick clouds caused people to lose their way along roads they had traveled since childhood. Some people likened the dusters to the massive clouds of smoke from an oil fire. A dust storm could last anything from an hour to three days. Borne on sixty-mile-an-hour winds, the dust invaded every crack in a house, filtering in through door and window casings, through keyholes, and down chimneys, to settle on the food a farm family had been hard pressed to gather. Respiratory diseases, such as bronchitis, strep throat and a new illness dubbed "dust pneumonia," sprang up throughout the region and, added to the malnutrition most farm families already suffered, these diseases proved deadly. Livestock also had little chance of surviving a large dust storm, especially since they too were undernourished because of their owners' inability to buy feed.

Some writers argue that the dust storms were caused by the Midwestern farmers themselves. Over a fifty-year period, farmers had stripped the land of its natural grasses and destroyed its surface layer with their steel plows. Without its natural protective covering, the dirt took to the skies, carried by westerly winds that swept through the Great Plains and propelled dust as far east as 300 miles out into the Atlantic Ocean.

Other writers blame only the lack of rainfall and cite evidence of a severe drought in the Midwest between 1200 and 1400 A.D. That drought killed off many plant and animal species and drove the Indians off the plains. The 1890s also saw a severe drought in the region, but from 1900 to 1930 the area had received more rainfall than normal. During the first thirty years of the century, the Great Plains, from Canada to Texas, were covered with wheat. It was Midwestern wheat that fed the Allied troops in World War I. Their work was grueling, but Midwestern farmers believed that their situation was improving yearly.

The drought hit these farmers hard. During the previous, more prosperous years, they had invested

LEFT: Clyde Hostetter, a farmer in St. Joe County, Indiana, displayed his corn crop, stunted by the severe drought, for a photographer in 1934.

ABOVE: Hills of sand in the Cimarron River Valley in western Oklahoma in March 1935. Throughout the region, the once fertile soil was blown away by high winds.

their profits in down payments on new farm equipment, such as tractors, disk plows, and combines. However, now that the war was over and European nations could rely once again on their own farm produce, Midwestern farmers saw their market decline. By the end of 1930, a million farm families in thirty states feared the lean years to come.

At the beginning of 1931, farmers in England, Arkansas, had had enough. Their children were hungry, and there was no relief in sight. On January 3, an armed band of 500 marched to the American Red Cross office and demanded food. Denied aid by the local authority, the farmers then approached grocers who, faced with shotguns and rifles, quietly doled out provisions. Later that month, another armed group invaded city hall in Oklahoma City. Police quickly cleared the group and jailed all the men.

From May 9-12, 1934, a giant duster swept through the plains, from North Dakota to Texas. Borne on 100-mile-an-hour winds, dust flew eastward as far as the Atlantic Coast. However, many Great Plains residents who lived through the 1930s believe that the duster on April 14, 1935, was the worst of any that decade. Beginning in eastern Wyoming, the storm sped along to the south through Colorado, Kansas, Oklahoma, and Texas. People caught outside in the storm, which raged at eighty miles an hour in Guymon, Oklahoma, fled wildly to any shelter they could find, including overturned cars or wagons and nearby cellars.

The Red Cross provided relief, including thousands of dust masks, for the area, but with the depression, the agency's funds had dwindled. Hungry Midwesterners received ten cents a day for food – only a third as much as was spent in some prisons to feed convicts.

In 1934, the federal government provided the drought-stricken areas with relief packages totaling 275 million dollars for cattlemen and 125 million dollars for farmers. In addition, the government sent agents to the area to spread word of a technique that would save the soil from further erosion. Farmers used listers, plow-like farm implements, to dig furrows in the soil and create ridges that would slow erosion. Dust Bowl farmers listed about eight million acres of land from July 1936 to July 1937. They received twenty cents an acre from the government for listing their own land or forty cents an acre if they hired others to do the job.

President Roosevelt set up some of his "alphabet soup" agencies with the drought-stricken farmers in mind. The Farm Security Administration was created to help half a million farmers relocate to more productive land. It was actually able to help only 4,500. The Agricultural Assistance Administration paid farmers not to produce crops, thereby driving the price of produce higher on the market.

In addition, President Roosevelt sent the Civilian Conservation Corps to the area to plant trees and to dam up rivers and streams. The CCC planted 200 million trees along a thousand-mile belt to slow the killer winds and storms. The dams helped the areas in which they were located by slowing the path of water into rivers and streams, but funds were not available to finance dams in every area.

LEFT: Dust storms could last three or four days, and the winds that bore the black clouds raged as fast as a hundred miles an hour. Dust filtered through door and window frames, keyholes, and chimneys, covering everything inside with a layer of dirt.

RIGHT: An abandoned farmhouse in Dalhart, Texas. Farmers throughout the Midwest and the Great Plains left their homes as conditions became too hard to bear in the 1930s. Often they moved to California, where they found seasonal employment as migrant agricultural workers.

Despite government aid, millions of Midwesterners headed west, becoming "exodusters" or "Okies." In South Dakota, the population declined by just over seven percent during the 1930s. Across the plains, abandoned houses and farmsteads dotted the landscape, an unnerving reminder to those who remained that they were but a hair's breadth from being "dusted out" themselves. Heavily in debt, due to their purchases of new farm equipment in the previous decade, farmers faced foreclosures. Some waited for county officials to serve foreclosure notices before leaving their homes. Others took to the roads without saying goodbye to friends who remained. In 1933, more than three billion dollars' worth of farmland, representing five percent of the nation's farms, was disposed of in forced sales.

Once the exodusters arrived in the west, they found employment in the huge agribusinesses that were developing in the area. However, unlike their year-round work back home, the new work was seasonal. In California, the exodusters picked lettuce, peaches, prunes, lemons, oranges, asparagus, cotton, and flax, but only for as long as there were crops in the fields to be

BELOW: Dusters hit the Great Plains and the Midwest throughout the 1930s. Thousands of people contracted various respiratory diseases, including strep throat and dust pneumonia.

RIGHT: An enterprising Little Rock, Arkansas, resident placed a "for sale" sign on the dry bed of the Arkansas River. In past years, the river had flooded many times, but in August 1934, it was completely dry.

picked. Once one job was finished, the exodusters moved on to another farm where ripening produce held the promise of a few more dollars.

In 1937, much of the Great Plains area saw the return of rain to the parched farmlands. Farmers who had managed to hang on felt saved. Unfortunately, drought never remains at bay for long. In the 1950s, the 1970s, and the 1980s, plains farmers suffered inadequate rainfall over a period of years. Yet they still endure. Sometimes the dust and wind are so bad that farmers wear ski masks as they cross their fields by tractor. They have also adopted new methods of irrigation and plowing, such as giant center-pivot irrigation fields that Easterners marvel at from west-bound airplanes.

No one knows the number of people who died in the raging dust storms of the 1930s. More easily documented are both the massive uprooting of the population and the number of acres abandoned. Nearly three and a half million people left their homes in the Great Plains as their once fertile fields blew into the skies, and nine million acres of farmland remained fallow for years to come.

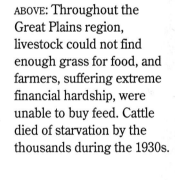

ABOVE: Throughout the Great Plains region, livestock could not find enough grass for food, and farmers, suffering extreme financial hardship, were unable to buy feed. Cattle died of starvation by the thousands during the 1930s.

LEFT: Dust and dirt piled up in high drifts after a particularly harsh dust storm. On a western Oklahoma farm in April 1935, a ridge of dirt reached almost as high as the barns.

CHAPTER THREE
STORMS

All disasters are relative, and
storms are no exception. The storm you lived through was always the worst.
You experienced the terror of sitting in total darkness as howling winds swept
through the nighttime skies; you watched helplessly as friends or relations
were pushed along the storm's destructive path; you waited impatiently for
food, water, or doctors to arrive on the scene. The people who lived through
the storms described below would disagree with you – and they would be right.
The Northeast blizzard of 1888, the Midwestern tornado of 1925, the South
Florida hurricanes of 1926 and 1928, and the Galveston hurricane of 1900 were
some of the worst storms America has ever seen either before or since.

LEFT: A worker clearing train tracks in New York. When the New York blizzard ended on March 14, 1888, the locals began digging out. By Friday, March 16, the transportation system was operating again

RIGHT: Luxury vacation homes on the Isle of Palms, South Carolina, represent just a fraction of those damaged by Hurricane Hugo as it passed over on September 22, 1989.

THE NORTHEAST BLIZZARD 1888

Most blizzards in the United States hit the Great Plains. They occur when very moist, warm air from the Gulf and cold arctic air collide, causing the warm air to ride up over the cold. When this happens, the moisture in the warm air condenses rapidly, causing snow to fall. All the conditions were right for a blizzard to occur in March 1888, but this one was not to be over the Great Plains; instead, the collision of air masses took place over the eastern seaboard. The blizzard that followed left heavy snowfalls from Massachusetts south to Washington, D.C. It also left around 400 people dead.

On Saturday, March 10, the weather in New York City was mild, almost springlike, with temperatures in the 50s, but the U.S. Weather Bureau predicted light snow for the following day. Instead, Northeasterners saw rain on the Sunday but, as temperatures fell that night, and as the wind picked up speed, a full-fledged storm was in the making.

Sailors at sea suffered from the blinding water spray kicked up by the wind. Several ships, such as the luxury yacht *Cythera*, sank, taking all aboard to their deaths. The crew of the *Niagara*, a freighter that had just returned from Havana, reported that the ship's decks were knee-deep in snow. In the Chesapeake Bay, a hundred vessels were lost, and in New York Harbor, thirty-three ships sank.

Snow began falling in New York City around midnight. Areas that had flooded earlier in the day due to heavy rains now froze solid. By the time New York's work force awoke on Monday morning, snow lay in a thick blanket all over the city. Those who decided to go to work that day faced extreme difficulties. The Brooklyn Bridge was closed due to ice-coated cables and the eighty-mile-an-hour winds that were howling over it. The ferries that normally plied the waters between Brooklyn and Manhattan were unable to make the crossing. Pedestrians had to contend with the danger of electrocution from stepping on fallen electrical, telegraph, and telephone wires. Then, there was the wind. Strong gusts whirled the snow before the faces of pedestrians, blinding them and causing them to lose their way along normally familiar streets. *The New York Times* reported that it took three hours to walk from 23rd Street to the downtown area, but that, even so, walking was faster than taking the elevated trains.

Most business operations remained closed for the day. At the New York Stock Exchange, thirty-three out of 1,100 employees arrived for work but, since the ticker tape worked only in spurts and because no senior managers were present to approve transactions, the stock exchange closed. This was the first time in more

BELOW: On March 12, 1888, residents of New York City and the surrounding area awoke to find a massive blizzard raging outside their homes. High winds and drifts of snow, as deep as eighteen feet in places, made walking in the streets nearly impossible.

LEFT: A drawing by W.P. Snyder depicting the rescue of a child during the March 1888 blizzard in New York.

RIGHT: A Manhattan street blanketed with two feet of snow that fell in the March 1888 blizzard. After the terrible storm, New York City officials sped up their efforts to finance the placement of electrical wires underground.

than a hundred years that the exchange had closed due to bad weather. The only comparable event was in 1881 when a severe sleet storm knocked down telegraph wires, delaying but not suspending trade.

By early afternoon, snow lay in a blanket nearly two feet thick, and drifts measuring eighteen feet deep further increased the danger of being out in the streets. Cabbies charged outrageous fees for use of their horse-drawn vehicles. Those who could not afford the going rate of 40 dollars per mile, took to the streets on foot where many fainted in the frigid air. Others died from heart failure, within hours or sometimes days of their strenuous march through the cold, wind, and snow. Earlier in the day, a train on the Third Avenue Elevated rear-ended another that had stalled on the tracks, leaving one person dead and injuring fourteen others. By afternoon all the elevated trains had stopped working. Passengers aboard the stranded trains found themselves freezing high above the streets as the wind howled past them. Some escaped by climbing across ladders stretched between the train and the upper floor of a nearby building, while the wind swirled blinding clouds of snow around them.

Grand Central Terminal closed at 3.00 p.m. Forty trains had been scheduled to arrive in New York City that day, but only two managed to get through the blizzard. Drifts and frozen switches made it impossible for the trains to run, and passengers were trapped without water, sanitary facilities, or food. Most

passengers stayed on board the trains, which were stuck along three major lines into the city; some were there for two days before help arrived. Some of those who decided to walk disappeared into drifts as they lost their way in the swirling snow.

That afternoon, hotels, restaurants, and bars throughout the city filled with people who were unable to make their way home. Some bars ran out of liquor. At Macy's, female clerks positioned mattresses and cots along the showroom floor and slept there for the night. The Custom House, the Clearing House, and the Sub-Treasury all closed their doors. In Albany, the state assembly adjourned when only twenty members arrived for the day's session. But P.J. Barnum's show went on, playing to only a hundred New Yorkers on the night of March 12.

On March 14, the storm abated. According to the New York Weather Station's meaurements, New Yorkers had been hit with almost twenty-one inches of snow, but the high winds had blown the snow into drifts as deep as fifty feet. Elsewhere in the Northeast, people fared no better than those in New York. Massachusetts and Connecticut reported drifts sixty feet deep, and people had to dig tunnels from their doorways up and out to the street. Twenty-two people drowned in Lewes, Delaware, when the high winds hurled the sea over dozens of boats docked in the harbor. Frozen bodies turned up throughout the spring, as drifts melted and as the waters of the Atlantic Ocean washed corpses to the shore.

THE MIDWEST TORNADOES 1925

Their sound, like hundreds of locomotives bearing down; their speed, sometimes measured as high as 300 miles an hour; and the destruction left in their wake all combine to make tornadoes terrifying experiences for those caught near them. The single most deadly tornado in America's history happened on March 18, 1925, in the Midwest. The black funnel killed 689 people, annihilated several towns in its path, and left millions of dollars of damage behind.

The majority of tornadoes occur in northern Texas, Oklahoma, Kansas, and southeast Nebraska, but areas of the Southeast are also susceptible. Certain weather conditions are required for tornadoes to occur. One theory involves the meeting of three air currents. Dry, cold polar air from Canada or the Rocky Mountains sweeps toward the south at speeds of fifty miles an hour, and then collides with moist tropical air of 75°F, which is moving northward. Added to these air masses are jet stream winds, moving eastward at 150 miles an hour. When the polar air collides with the tropical air, the colder air sweeps up over the warmer. The warm air eventually pushes up through the cold mass at great speeds, causing violent thunderstorms to occur. The jet stream plays a part by twisting the rising warm air into a whirling column, which then travels from southwest to northeast at speeds as fast as seventy miles an hour. The funnel measures between 800 and 2,000 feet high and is between 600 and 990 feet wide at the base.

On the afternoon of March 18, 1925, the U.S. Weather Bureau called for thunderstorms in Indiana, Illinois, and Kentucky. Lacking sophisticated satellites, high-altitude weather balloons, and other modern-day equipment, the Bureau had no inkling that a tornado was on its way. The funnel first touched down in Arkansas, but no extensive damage occurred there. Off it sped to Annapolis in southeastern Missouri. There it wiped out Main Street, knocking down every building along the road, including the railroad depot, where several people were trapped under the wreckage.

Cape Girardeau was the next place in the tornado's deadly path. Class had just let out when the funnel slammed into a public school. Moving in a northeasterly direction, the tornado then hit Murphysboro, Illinois, a town with 11,000 residents. Demolishing houses, ripping trees from the ground, and sucking automobiles up into its furious center, the storm killed some people immediately. Others died later in the fires that broke out throughout the town. That afternoon 210 people died in Murphysboro, and 500 were injured.

Increased in size and power, the tornado swept into De Soto, Illinois, a town of 600 people. Whole houses

RIGHT: In Frankfurt, Illinois, 197 people were killed in the March 1925 tornado, and the town was reduced to splinters.

LEFT: The ruins of Longfellow School, where sixty children were killed, in Murphysboro, Illinois. The town was in the path of the March 1925 tornado Another 150 people were killed elsewhere in the town.

BELOW: West Frankfurt, Illinois in the aftermatch of the March 1925 tornado, the deadliest in United States history. All along its path through Indiana, Missouri, Illinois, Kentucky, and Tennessee, the tornado left massive destruction, and 689 people were killed.

were lifted from their foundations up into the funnel, but the most horrifying destruction occurred when the tornado slammed into the town's public school. Unlike Cape Girardeau's students and teachers, those in De Soto were still in class that afternoon. First the roof of the building was ripped off, then the walls collapsed inward, trapping students and teachers under the wreckage. Rescuers hurried to free the children, but what they found was horrifying. Of the 125 people in the building, only thirty-seven survived. Elsewhere in De Soto, or what was left of it, buildings lay in ruins, and human bodies hung from trees and fences.

Further to the northeast, Frankfort, Illinois, was reduced to splinters in minutes, and 197 people lay dead.

Still the tornado whirled its way across the Midwest. Eleven more Illinois towns felt its fury before it moved into Indiana, hitting Princeton, Owensville, Griffin, Poseyville, and Elizabeth. Near Princeton, the tornado pulled four miners out of the car in which they were riding before crushing the car flat. All four men survived. Princeton's new Southern Railroad yard was ripped apart from end to end, and freight cars were tossed about in the air.

At the end of the afternoon, survivors in twenty-three cities and towns looked around them at millions of dollars' worth of damage and grieved for the 689 dead.

BELOW: A flattened Indiana landscape. Several towns in Indiana were hit by the March 1925 tornado before its fury was spent.

RIGHT: Another view of tornado damage in Indiana after the March 1925 funnel ripped through the Midwest.

BELOW RIGHT: An overall view of the devastation in Murphysboro, Illinois, after the March 1925 tornado.

MIAMI, FLORIDA 1926

Before the days when hurricanes were given names such as Agnes or Camille or Hugo, they were identified only by year. Mention the year 1926 to older South Floridians, and they will immediately recall that year's deadly storm.

The Miami Daily News warned its readers of an approaching storm on the afternoon of September 17, but the word "hurricane" was not used. Few people were disturbed by what editors were calling a "tropical storm." By the time the red and black hurricane flags were hoisted into Miami's skies, the storm was sweeping into the city. At its end around noon on September 18, 372 people had been killed and 2,000 people across the state had been injured.

Although not the strongest hurricane ever to hit Florida – it was rated as four on the five-point Saffir-Simpson hurricane scale – the 1926 hurricane proved deadly because people were unprepared. Today's sophisticated weather tracking systems warn seacoast residents of approaching hurricanes, and even young schoolchildren learn how to track hurricanes on maps available everywhere, from the sides of grocery bags to the backs of restaurant placemats. Once the Weather Service has determined the path of a hurricane, residents are warned either to evacuate the area or to board up the windows and doors of their houses.

Just before midnight on Friday, September 17, the hurricane made its way into Miami. At 6.10 a.m. on Saturday, the awesome winds died out, and people everywhere ran into the streets rejoicing that the storm had passed. Some people dressed in bathing suits and waded through the flood or ran to play on the beach. Unfortunately, the calm was only a lull in the storm; Miami at that time was actually centered under the eye of the hurricane. At 6.45 a.m., the storm struck again, with even greater fury than before, and thousands of Miamians were caught in the streets. Storm tides measuring eight to nine feet high poured over Miami Beach and into the city itself. By noon, Miami had weathered the worst of the storm, but now people to the north and west, in Hollywood, Fort Lauderdale, and Moore Haven, felt its fury.

On Saturday, Miami officials declared martial law and closed off access to the bridges and causeways entering the city in an attempt to keep sightseers at bay. Marines stationed at Key West and national guardsmen patrolled the streets for signs of looters.

LEFT: Wreckage left by the South Florida hurricane of 1926. Damage estimates in the Miami area reached $76 million; 5,000 homes were demolished.

RIGHT: Beach property in Palm Beach after the 1926 hurricane.

President Calvin Coolidge appealed for contributions for the hurricane victims on September 20, but the Red Cross noted something extremely odd about the flow of money. At first funds drifted in, then they stopped abruptly. It seems that officials in South Florida had decided that the publicity from a nationwide campaign would cripple the area's tourist industry. They issued statements that the damage was not as bad as had been reported and told mayors and governors of other areas that they would be notified if their help was needed. In all the Red Cross collected four million dollars, which was one million dollars short of the agency's estimate of the funds required.

Florida was not spared two years later when another hurricane struck Palm Beach and the Lake Okeechobee area. Palm Beach was nearly wiped out in the storm , but at Lake Okeechobee 1,800 people, mostly black itinerant workers, met their deaths. 5,000 workers were living in shacks and tents in the area and, when the 160-mile-an-hour winds blew water up over the levees, many of the workers took refuge in attics or on the roofs of buildings. Their night was filled with terror, as poisonous snakes crawled through the swampy Everglades to attack the weary survivors.

BELOW: The heart of Miami a week after the South Florida hurricane of September 1926. This was not the strongest hurricane ever to hit the area,but was deadly because people were unprepared for its fury. It struck Miami just before midnight on September 17, and continued until noon the next day.

RIGHT: Buena Vista Street, Miami. On the afternoon of Saturday, September 18, 1926, officials declared martial law in the city, and Miamians began clearing away debris.

BELOW: Damage caused in Miami. One reason the storm was so deadly was that thousands of people ran out into the street to celebrate its end on Saturday morning, September 1. However, far from being at an end, the eye of the storm was at that time centered over Miami. Moments later, the storm struck again, and people were caught outdoors in the howling wind. In Miami, 115 people were killed.

GALVESTON, TEXAS 1900

After the 1928 Florida hurricane came the 1935 hurricane in the Florida Keys, when hundreds of people working on the overseas highway to Key West were killed. In 1969 came hurricane Camille, causing one billion dollars' worth of damage along huge stretches of beach property in Alabama and Mississippi. Hurricane Agnes in 1972 killed 118 people and caused three billion dollars' worth of damage to property from northern Florida, through Virginia, Pennsylvania, and New York. Then in 1989, hurricane Hugo hit South Carolina and the historic city of Charleston with tremendous fury.

Yet none of these matched the destruction of the hurricane that annihilated Galveston, Texas, in 1900. In fact no other single American disaster of any kind has claimed as many lives as that deadly hurricane. When the death toll was finally calculated, an estimated 8,000 people had been killed.

Galveston is built on a sandy island about thirty miles long and about three miles wide. The highest point on the island was then about fifteen feet above the water level. In 1900, 37,000 people lived in the city, which was a major deep-water port, and the wealthiest city per capita in the Southwest.

The city received its first warning that a major storm was brewing on September 4, when the U.S. Weather Bureau reported a tropical storm headed toward Cuba. Over the next few days, the storm mounted, changing course now and then, until on Friday, September 17, it headed straight toward Galveston island. That morning, residents and vacationers were delighted to see the turbulent seas with huge dark waves breaking on the shore. Before long, though, the waves were spilling over into the city's streets. Despite the efforts of a Weather Bureau employee named Issac Cline, who rode up and down the beaches warning sightseers of the impending danger, the public stayed at the beach out of curiosity – at least until the Pagoda, a structure covering two blocks, was reduced to splinters in the crashing waves.

The hurricane-force winds rushed in by early afternoon. Throughout the city, pieces of slate roofing flew through the air, wounding or killing all those they struck. Water from the gulf blew across the streets, first knocking down the shacks and less substantial residences along the beach, then making its way toward the middle-class and wealthy sections behind the beach. Residents of the low-lying areas sought refuge in the more solidly built homes toward the center of town, and before long, everyone moved from first to second floors as the water grew deeper.

All over town houses began to crumble. People who

ABOVE: The 1900 hurricane either smashed boats in Galveston's harbor to splinters or tossed them about like toys. These boats were swept inland to the railyard, where they were left after the water receded.

LEFT: The Galveston hurricane of 1900 was by far the deadliest hurricane in the United States. An estimated 8,000 people were killed in Galveston and along the Texas coast. On Friday, September 17, the storm veered directly into Galveston Island, smashing everything in its path.

were not crushed by the falling debris fought their way, sometimes underwater, to floating rooftops, beams, or barrels – anything they could grab. Some spent several hours gripping trees. One group found a floating cistern, climbed in, and bobbed along through the night.

As the wind shifted direction, water from Galveston Bay met water from the Gulf of Mexico, and the entire island was submerged. Terrified families huddled in buildings that had somehow managed to remain standing. Nearly a thousand people crowded into Tremont Hotel, a hundred into Union Station, and a few dozen into Lucas Terrace apartment building. At Saint Mary's Infirmary, people fought their way through water that was then knee-deep and later became five feet deep to take refuge in the hospital building. Because of the howling wind, which was estimated to be between 110 and 120 miles an hour at times, few people heard the crash of the two-ton bell that fell from Saint Mary's Cathedral or the splintering of the 200-foot-tall spire of Saint Patrick's Church.

RIGHT: One Galveston school was swept off its foundations and carried for 600 feet during the 1900 hurricane.

BELOW: On the morning of September 18, 1900, Galvestonians emerged from their hiding places to face a horrific sight. All about them lay the dead. Nearly half the buildings on the island were utterly destroyed.

The storm tide rose to just over fifteen feet. At Saint Mary's Orphanage, the nuns, hoping to keep the children within reach, tied the orphans together with a clothesline. However, the building could not withstand the crashing wind and water. Around 7.00 or 8.00 p.m. that evening, the roof caved in. Only three orphans out of ninety survived.

At Bolivar Lighthouse, across the mouth of Galveston Bay on Bolivar Peninsula, about fifty people huddled together, moving as a group up the stairs of the lighthouse as the water level rose. The lighthouse withstood the storm but, when the waters receded and people could leave their cramped refuge, they saw the bodies of several people who had tried to make their way to the building littered about the grounds.

The hurricane flattened the Old Women's Home, killing everyone inside. It ripped the iron roof off Union Station. It left only one room of the sixty-four-room Lucas Terrace apartment building standing.

At midnight, the storm lessened. The next morning, survivors crept from their hiding places and looked around. Half of the buildings were annihilated. Nearly every house in town that still stood had suffered heavy damage. The bodies of dead animals and people, thousands of them, lay everywhere.

Galveston had no electricity, water, food, or medical supplies, and no way to call the outside world for help. Mayor Walter C. Jones called emergency meetings twice that day to begin organizing a relief committee. First, the committee sent a group of men across the bay on the *Pherabe*, one of the only boats still seaworthy, to get help. Mayor Jones swore in several men as temporary policemen to patrol the streets for looters. That same afternoon, the townspeople began searching for bodies.

They did not have to look very hard at first. Bodies lay everywhere, especially around the rubble of buildings. Given the hot September sun, the townspeople knew that they had to dispose of the bodies quickly. Volunteers and others who had been conscripted at gunpoint loaded bodies onto a barge docked at the 12th Street wharf. By Monday evening, the end of the first full day of searching, the barge held 700 bodies, and late that night crews floated the barge out to sea and dumped the weighted corpses into the water.

The next morning, Galvestonians witnessed another horrifying sight. Many of the bodies had been dumped into the sea without sufficient weight, and they had simply floated back to the shore.

Galveston had always been plagued by yellow fever, and now city officials were terrified that an epidemic would break out if the bodies were not disposed of quickly. They decided to cremate those on the shore. As others turned up amid the rubble, they were either buried in shallow graves or burned. Throughout the fall, Galvestonians found more and more of the dead. Even years later, beachcombers would sometimes come across skeletons buried in the sand.

As reports of the devastation in Galveston circulated in the nation's newspapers, contributions flowed in from private individuals, from companies, and from whole towns. Johnstown, Pennsylvania, having lost 2,209 of its citizens in the flood of 1889, immediately went to work raising money for Galveston. Andrew Carnegie donated 20,000 dollars. Contributions totaled two and a half million dollars. Red Cross founder Clara Barton, aged seventy-eight, rushed to the disaster scene. Relief for Galveston was the last disaster effort headed by Barton. For two months, she organized relief volunteers, surveyed survivors to determine their most pressing needs, and distributed money, clothing, food, and building supplies.

As a result of the deadly 1900 hurricane, three permanent changes were made in the city of Galveston. First, a sea wall that ran for six miles along the gulf was constructed. Built of concrete and with creosote pilings driven deep into the sand, the wall stood seventeen feet above the average low-tide level. Completed in 1904, the sea wall protected Galveston from the fourteen-foot-high tide of a tropical storm in 1915.

The second change was that made to Galveston's level. Four years after the storm, a 300-foot-wide, twenty-foot-deep canal was dug through the city's center.

Dredges pulled sand up from the Gulf floor and pumped it into the areas to be raised. Workers had to jack up more than 2,000 buildings and move hundreds of others out of the path of the canal diggers. By 1910, the city of Galveston had been raised to a height of seventeen feet near the sea wall.

The last change was that made to the government of Galveston. Before the storm, a mayor and an alderman representing twelve wards governed the city. When Mayor Jones called the emergency meetings at the Tremont Hotel and assigned individuals to head specific relief operations, he had hit on an idea that served Galveston well. Galveston worked out a new charter based on this concept, and the city became the first in the country to be governed by commissioners, each being responsible for a separate city function.

BELOW: Galveston men were sworn in as temporary policemen after the hurricane. Their job entailed not only keeping the peace and preventing looting, but also searching for the bodies of the victims.

RIGHT: At 3.30 p.m. on September 17, 1938, the Great New England Hurricane ripped through Long Island, New York. An eighteen-foot wave smashed into the shore, killing several swimmers. An aerial view of the bay near Westhampton, Long Island, shows a house that was swept off its foundations during the storm.

LEFT: An automobile that toppled into the breach of a bridge broken by the Great New England Hurricane.

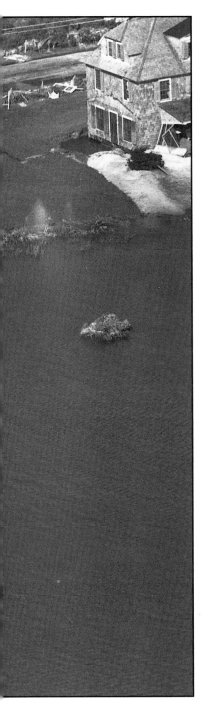

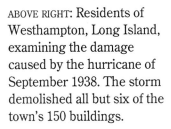

ABOVE RIGHT: Residents of Westhampton, Long Island, examining the damage caused by the hurricane of September 1938. The storm demolished all but six of the town's 150 buildings.

RIGHT: The Great New England Hurricane aggravated already overflowing rivers, bringing torrential rains, and causing devastating floods.

ABOVE: The 1938 hurricane struck New England's shoreline at 186 miles an hour causing severe damage, as here in Falmouth, Massachusetts.

LEFT: More than 400 people died under the combined pressure of hurricane and floods in New England in September 1938, and thousands more were injured. An injured woman is being rushed on a stretcher to a first aid station in Waterville, Massachusetts.

LEFT: On April 6, 1936, a tornado that hit the southern United States broke gas mains and electrical lines in Gainesville, Georgia, causing several fires in the town, and annihilating 630 buildings.

BELOW: A new school in Tupelo, Mississippi, was wrecked by the April 1936 tornado. Throughout the city, 195 people were killed, and damage estimated at $4 million was caused.

ABOVE: Convicts working at
the demolished Pruitt and
Barrett Hardware Company
on the town squarein
Gainesville, Georgia,
clearing up after the April
1936 tornado.

BELOW: Hurricane Camille struck the Gulf Coast of the United States in August 1969. More than 250 people died during the storm and property damage estimated at $1 billion was inflicted. The Biloxi, Mississippi, church, at left, was split in two by the tremendously high winds. Thousands of people were left homeless in the region.

RIGHT: While Mobile, Alabama, did not suffer a great deal of wind damage during Hurricane Camille in August 1969, the town's waterfront area was swept over by high tides.

BELOW: Hurricane Hazel struck western Haiti on October 12, 1954, killing 100 people. It then headed north, smashing into Myrtle Beach, South Carolina, on October 15, and rushing on toward North Carolina. Shown here is a destroyed tobacco warehouse in Wallace, North Carolina.

RIGHT: The water in the Potomac River rose far above normal when Hurricane Hazel smashed into Washington, D.C. Park policemen, such as this man at Hains Point, kept a close watch on the water level.

RIGHT: Fallen trees littered Capitol Plaza in Washington, D.C., after Hurricane Hazel swept over the city.

LEFT: Hurricane Hazel rammed into Washington, D.C., with 50- to 60-mile-an-hour winds on October 15, 1954.

RIGHT: After Washington, D.C., Hurricane Hazel made its way up the coast, through Maryland, Delaware, New Jersey, and New York. Shown here is the damaged boardwalk at Atlantic Beach, New Jersey. The hurricane then moved inland toward the Great Lakes, and ripped through Toronto, killing fifty-six people.

RIGHT: Hurricane Hugo struck South Carolina on September 22, 1989, blowing out of commission the only bridge connecting Charleston on the mainland with Sullivans Island.

BELOW: When Hurricane Hugo hit Myrtle Beach, South Carolina, on September 22, 1989, it destroyed homes and covered the roads with sand.

RIGHT: An aerial view of the drawbridge that links Charleston, South Carolina, with Sullivans Island after Hurricane Hugo had passed over in 1989.

LEFT: Christiansted, St. Croix, in the U.S. Virgin Islands was almost demolished by Hurricane Hugo, which struck on September 18, 1989. There was violent looting in the days that followed, prompting the government to ask from help from the U.S. to control the violence.

RIGHT: After several days of disorder, residents begin to rebuild houses in Christiansted, St. Croix, following the havoc wreaked by Hurricane Hugo.

BELOW: Hurricane Hugo lifted yachts onto the water front in Christiansted, St. Croix. The island was without water or electricity following the storm.

CHAPTER FOUR

FIRES

Fire and the destruction it brings have been a constant cause of fear for city dwellers worldwide. In America's past, major fires have taken the lives of untold people, some while enjoying cocktails and conversation, as happened at Boston's Cocoanut Grove nightclub in November 1942 and at the Beverly Hills Country Club in Southgate, Kentucky, in May 1977, others while watching performances, as happened at Hartford, Connecticut's Ringling Brothers and Barnum and Bailey Circus at the Barbour Street show grounds where 168 people died in July 1944 and at Richmond Theater in December 1811 where seventy people were killed. On February 7 and 8, 1904, Baltimore was consumed by a fire that destroyed the entire business district and caused some eighty-five million dollars' worth of damage. Remarkably, only one person was killed in this conflagration, which destroyed 2,500 buildings. On November 8, 1872, sixty-five acres in the heart of Boston's business district were destroyed by a fire that caused some seventy-five million dollars' worth of damage to property and killed twelve people. On March 21, 1788, New Orleans caught fire when a candle was knocked over in the home of Don Vincente Nunez. In only five hours, 856 buildings were destroyed and scores of people were killed.

On October 8, 1871, fierce winds fed the flames of logging fires in eastern Wisconsin. Four hundred square miles of countryside were destroyed, 750 people died from suffocation, and another 750 people burned to death. In the town of Peshtigo, half the residents were killed. The winds that swept across the drought-stricken Midwest through Peshtigo also contributed to the most famous fire of all. The Chicago Fire began the same night that Peshtigo was annihilated by flames. From Sunday, October 8, until Tuesday, October 10, 1871, a giant conflagration destroyed 200 million dollars' worth of property and killed some 300 people living in the Windy City.

RIGHT: A fire at the Standard Oil Company's plant in Cleveland, Ohio, on September 7, 1944, was fought by workmen in a bucket brigade, using chemicals.

THE CHICAGO FIRE 1871

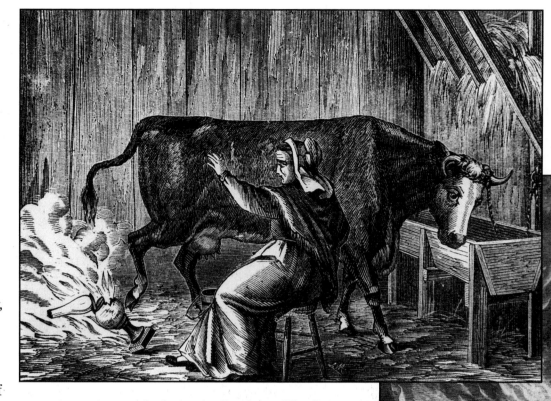

In 1871, Chicago was a thriving city of 300,000 people. Less than forty years before, when Chicago was formally organized, fewer than 100 people lived there. Since then, Chicago had grown into a mighty transportation center. Everyday more than 200 freight and passenger trains ran through the city's great railyard, and traders also used the Great Lakes and the Chicago River to transport materials.

Chicago was neatly divided into three sections by the river, which forked about half a mile inland from Lake Michigan's shore. Chicago's South Side, that section of town between the lake and the southern fork of the river, was home to both the central business section and the city's squalid slums. The North Side, that section between the lake and the northern fork of the river, boasted the city's most splendid houses and mansions. The West Side, the section of the city west of the forks of the river, was home to Chicago's working classes and to several new industries. Twelve pivoting wooden bridges spanned the river, and connected the three sections of the city.

For three months before the great Chicago fire, little rain had fallen. The first week of October had also been abnormally warm. The city of wooden business establishments, homes, barns, and fences, 651 miles of raised wooden sidewalks, and fifty-six miles of streets paved with wooden blocks had been reduced to a tinderbox. A week before the great fire, a warehouse on 16th Street had burned down. The day before the city was consumed, a West Side planing mill on Canal Street went up in flames, and these spread to nearby buildings. In the four-block area consumed by the fire, about 750,000 dollars' worth of damage was caused to property. Fighting the blaze for sixteen hours, Chicago's firemen at last brought the fire under control, but not before some of the department's firefighting equipment had been destroyed.

On October 8, at about 8.45 p.m., another blaze started, and this time the exhausted fire department was unable to restrict it to the West Side barn in which it started. No one knows the exact cause of the blaze. Legend has it that one of Mrs. Patrick O'Leary's cows kicked over a lantern while being milked, but Mrs. O'Leary swore that neither she nor her family was in the barn when the fire broke out. Another possibility is that one of Mrs. O'Leary's boarders, Dennis "Peg Leg" Sullivan slipped into the barn for a quick sip of liquor and accidentally set the barn on fire while lighting his pipe.However, Sullivan, too, swore that he was nowhere near the barn when the blaze started. Whatever the cause of the blaze, its fury was heightened by some critical mistakes made during its first hour. The first alarm, sent out at about 9.00 p.m., did not reach the courthouse where the city maintained its telegraph fire alarm system. A few minutes later, the watchman on duty in the courthouse saw the fire but thought it was of no significance. Only at about 9.30 p.m. did he realize that the fire was spreading and help was needed, but he misjudged the location of the fire and sounded the wrong alarm.

It was not until nearly three quarters of an hour after the fire started that the first firefighting equipment sped up DeKoven Street where the O'Learys lived. A mild wind thwarted the firemen's efforts and sent sparks flying everywhere. At 10.00 p.m., sparks landed on the steeple of St. Paul's Church, five blocks north of DeKoven Street. Next to the church was a furniture-finishing factory. Once the fire spread to this, the building's contents – paints, varnishes, and other highly combustible materials – caught fire in a roar, and, from then on, the blaze was out of control.

Around midnight, strong southwest winds pushed the fire across the Chicago River into the South Side. First it consumed the Parmelee Omnibus and Stage Company, and then moved quickly into Conley's Patch, a slum filled with insubstantial wooden shacks and saloons. By 1.30 a.m., the entire business section was burning. The post office, the courthouse, the customs house, Crosby's Opera House, and the Field & Lieter dry goods store were all consumed in the blaze.

On Monday morning, the fire jumped the river into Chicago's North Side. Residents leaped from their beds, gathered what few belongings they could carry, and rushed away from their houses and the possessions accumulated over a lifetime. Fire devils –searingly hot

LEFT: Legend has it that the Great Chicago Fire of 1871 was caused when Mrs. O'Leary's cow kicked over an oil lamp in the family's barn. No matter what the cause, the fire devastated the city, which was built of wood at the time.

BELOW: An engraving from a sketch by John R. Chapin, showing the rush of people across Randolph Street Bridge during the 1871 Chicago fire.

air combined with whirling flames – jumped from one building to the next. As people rushed through the streets, burning timbers and shingles fell about them. Choking on smoke, they ran to the homes of friends in areas as yet untouched by the fire or to Lincoln Park, where they found refuge in the grave sites that had only recently been emptied when the city relocated its cemetery to another area.

Some of Chicago's residents managed to find horse-drawn wagons and carts to transport their household belongings away from the fire area. Others were only able to save what they could carry in bundles. Sometimes people were even forced to abandon what little they had saved when sparks flying through the air landed on the bundles and ignited them. If time allowed, some residents buried belongings, such as family silver, pianos, and other pieces of furniture too large to move, in their yards, but when they returned to the smouldering ashes that had been their homes, they found that their treasures had burned in the ground.

The fire raged on, until around 11.00 p.m. on October 9, when the winds abated and a light rain began falling, slowly quenching the smoldering city. The area destroyed by the fire ran for nearly five miles to the north and south and was about one mile wide. Within this area, 196 million dollars' worth of property was destroyed, and some 300 people were killed. Exact fatality figures were never calculated, and it is assumed that many bodies were never recovered from the ruined buildings.

Chicagoans began rebuilding their city with amazing speed. Only a few weeks after the fire, some 200 new buildings were under construction in the South Side. A month after the fire, homeless Chicagoans found shelter in 5,000 newly constructed houses that the Chicago Relief and Aid Society had constructed and furnished. A year later, new buildings worth forty million dollars had been built throughout the city.

ABOVE: Throughout the burning area, Chicagoans hurried to gather what few valuables they could before fleeing from their homes to escape the flames.

LEFT: At the junction of the Chicago River, the flames spread, destroying shipping and grain elevators.

RIGHT: Two days after the fire started in Chicago, *The New York Times* carried this map of the burned area, and almost the entire front page was devoted to news about the fire.

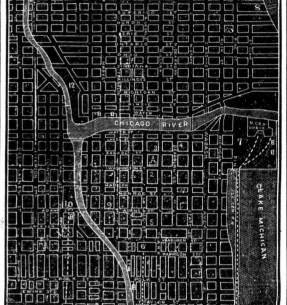

BELOW: An 1871 woodcut depicts Chicagoans laying the cornerstone of the first building to be constructed after the fire. Chicago developers rebuilt the city with amazing speed. Within a year, $40-million-worth of new construction had been completed or was underway.

RIGHT: Chicago in ruins after the 1871 fire. In the city, 90,000 people were left homeless.

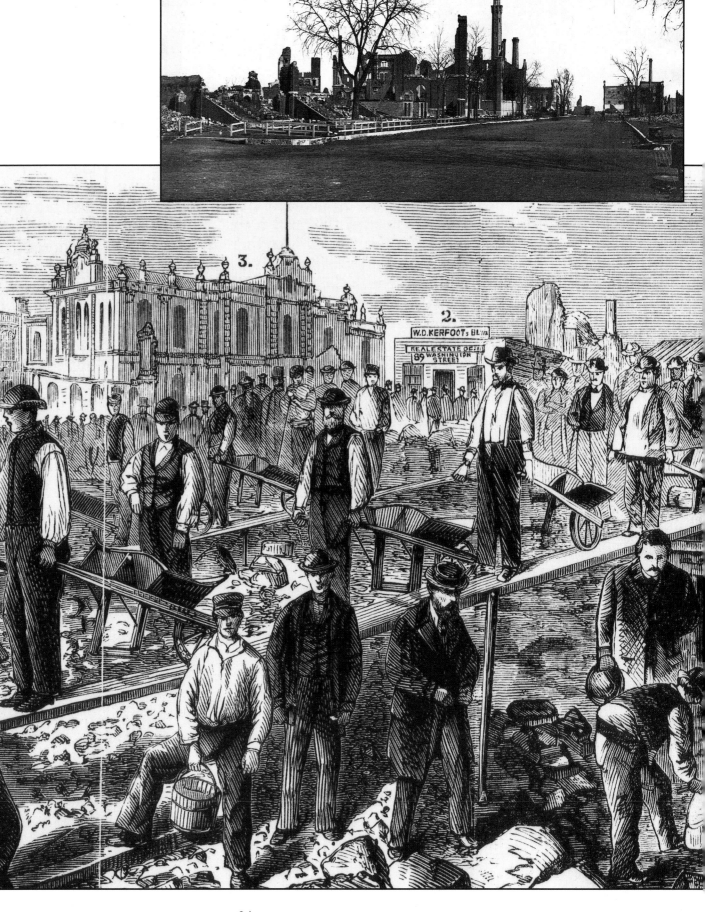

BELOW RIGHT: After the fire, the Field & Seiter dry goods store lay in smoldering ruins. A sign instructs employees to collect their wages at another site.

RIGHT: The Great Chicago Fire caused property damage totaling $196 million and killed about 300 of Chicago's population of 300,000. An 1871 woodcut depicts survivors carrying on their lives in the midst of the ruined city.

ABOVE: From February 7-8, 1904, fire raged through Baltimore, Maryland, causing property damage totaling $85 million. The fire started in a dry goods warehouse and spread over 140 acres. While 2,500 buildings were consumed by flames, only one person was killed.

RIGHT: Workers clearing away debris resulting from the fire in Baltimore, Maryland, in 1904. In terms of damage, the fire was the second largest in United States history. Only the Chicago fire of 1871 was larger.

LEFT: Bystanders line the outer edges of charred cattle pens to watch the fire that raged through several square blocks of stockyards at Cleveland, Ohio, in March 1944.

ABOVE: As well as cattle, two firemen perished in Cleveland's 1944 stockyard fire.

ABOVE: A Port Chicago, California, resident holding a shell that ripped through the walls of his home after the explosions on board two ships in the harbor on July 17, 1944.

RIGHT: The hulls of the two munitions ships, the *Quinault Victory* and the *E.A. Bryan*, protrude from the water after the explosion of their cargoes of TNT and cordite in July 1944 at Port Chicago, California. The explosion killed 321 men who were working on the docks.

LEFT: Pieces of the two wrecked ships littered the ruined dock in Port Chicago. The cause of the explosion was never determined. Some blamed it on part of the cargo – ammunition left over from World War I. People fifty miles away saw flames leaping into the sky.

BELOW: Twenty miles away from the explosion in Port Chicago, California, buildings suffered broken windows and other damage. Two miles from the explosion site, three men attempt to dislodge a huge chunk of one of the ship's decks from a concrete sidewalk.

ABOVE: Property damage totaled more than $100 million in Texas City after the April 16, 1947, explosion of two ships in the city's harbor. The giant Monsanto chemical plant, near the explosion's site, was completely destroyed.

LEFT: At 9:12 a.m. on April 16, 1947, in the harbor of Texas City, Texas, 2,300 tons of highly combustible fertilizer ignited in the hold of the *Grandcamp.* The nearby *Highflyer,* loaded with sulphur and ammonium, caught fire the next day. As a result, 552 people died.

RIGHT: The section of ship in the foreground was blown out of the harbor in Texas City when the *Grandcamp*'s combustible cargo exploded.

ABOVE: The ruins of an enormous warehouse near the harbor in Texas City. A third of the buildings in the town were destroyed in the spreading fire.

RIGHT: Some of the 3,000 people injured in the Texas City explosion were transported to Houston where the City Auditorium was turned into a temporary hospital.

FAR RIGHT: A year after the disaster in Texas City and reconstruction is under way.

LEFT: Some of the Cocoanut Grove's patrons escaped through a side door when the fire broke out. Others climbed onto the roof and descended a ladder. Inside, guests stampeded their way to safety. The two-story club was filled with flammable materials, including cloth ceilings, leather-covered walls, and artificial plants.

BELOW: Victims of the tragic fire at Cocoanut Grove nightclub lay dead, dying, or injured on the sidewalk outside the building.

LEFT: On November 28, 1942, nearly a thousand merrymakers crowded into Boston's Cocoanut Grove, a popular nightclub. Suddenly, a chorus girl ran screaming through the club, her hair on fire. The entire nightclub was soon in flames. The fire killed 491 people and injured hundreds more.

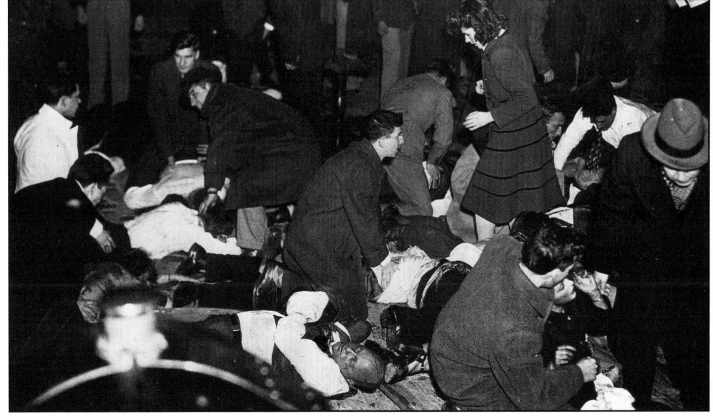

LEFT: The main dining room of Cocoanut Grove in ruins after the November 28, 1942, fire.

ABOVE: The day after the fire, charred tables and chairs were piled up inside the Cocoanut Grove club.

LEFT: Thirty-five years after the devastation at Cocoanut Grove in Boston, a fire at another nightclub, the Beverly Hills Supper Club in Southgate, Kentucky, brought death to 165 people. As firemen climb ladders to fight the blaze, the bodies of some of the victims lie on the hillside.

RIGHT: An aerial view of the Beverly Hills Supper Club after the fire. Victims' families sought damages of more than $2 billion.

BELOW: The shell of the Beverly Hills Supper Club the day after the flash fire of May 1977.

BELOW RIGHT: Normally used for weddings, one small chapel became a morgue on the night of the Beverly Hills Supper Club fire.

CHAPTER FIVE

BUILDING COLLAPSE

As workers were pouring the concrete roof onto a five-story condominium building in Cocoa Beach, Florida, on March 27, 1981, the roof on which they were standing suddenly caved in. Eleven construction workers were killed, and fourteen were injured as each floor fell onto the next. On June 4, 1979, the roof on the Kemper Arena in Kansas City, Missouri, collapsed after a huge downpour coupled with unusually strong winds. No one was injured because the arena was not in use at the time. Had the storm hit three years earlier, the entire 1976 Republican Convention could have ended in massive numbers of injuries or deaths. As it was, the city had to spend one million dollars on repairs and lost just over one million dollars in rental, user, parking, and concession fees. Kansas City would not be so lucky when disaster struck again, two years after the Kemper Arena collapse.

LEFT: Nearly 1,000 rescue workers rushed to the scene of the Hyatt Regency Hotel disaster and worked all night trying to free people trapped under the debris of the fallen "skybridges." Whenever rescuers found a survivor, cheers rang out through the hotel lobby.

RIGHT: In Cocoa Beach, Florida, workers were pouring a concrete roof on the Harbor Cay condominium under construction when the five-story building suddenly collapsed on March 27, 1981. The top four floors of the structure dropped, one on top of the other, killing eleven workmen and injuring fourteen others.

THE KANSAS CITY HYATT REGENCY 1981

On July 17, 1981, about 1,500 people had thronged to the Kansas City Hyatt Regency for a tea dance featuring Steven Miller and his Orchestra. The dance floor itself, on which partygoers were fox-trotting to their hearts' content, was not large enough to hold everybody at one time. About 150 people were watching from the wings on two of the hotel's three skybridges. These 145-foot-long walkways spanned the lobby; one was four stories above the lobby floor, one was raised two stories, and another was raised three stories and projected fifteen feet farther out from the wall than the other two.

Suddenly, at 7.01 p.m., the band's strains of *Satin Doll* were interrupted by several loud cracks. The center section of the highest skybridge collapsed, crashing first into the lowest skybridge, and then plummeting to the lobby floor, leaving 150 people flailing about. Witnesses later said that, just before the loud crack, the upper skybridge began swaying slowly in time with the music. From the first awful crack to the last roaring boom, fifteen seconds elapsed.

The lucky people that night were those far away from the falling bridges, but even they had cuts and bruises from the flying glass and debris. The unlucky people were those dancing under or near the bridges. The two bridges cracked into four sections each. From piles of debris as high as six feet, the arms and legs of trapped people protruded.

Stunned by the horror around them, the uninjured were slow to call for help. A full three minutes passed before someone called the Kansas City Fire Department. Another three minutes passed before the first firetruck arrived. Thereafter, rescuers poured onto the scene. Construction workers from nearby sites rushed in with jackhammers and other equipment. In all, nearly a thousand rescuers helped to dig out the injured and dead. Firemen, policemen, doctors and nurses, and Red Cross and Salvation Army volunteers all pitched in for a long night of hard work.

At 9.30 p.m., a backhoe brought from a construction site knocked out the revolving doors of the hotel's lobby, and a crane crashed through the lobby's glass wall. The way was now clear for the heavy lifting equipment to enter the building.

Inch by inch, workers jackhammered through chunks of the broken skybridges, always taking care to avoid hitting anyone trapped below. Piece by piece, the workers lifted the wreckage away. What they found was sometimes horrific and sometimes miraculous. Some

BELOW: Firemen lifting an injured man out of the wreckage in the Hyatt Regency Hotel. The last ten survivors were found at 6:00 a.m. on the morning after the collapse.

RIGHT: On the evening of July 17, 1981, 1,500 people flocked to the Kansas City, Missouri, Hyatt Regency Hotel for a tea dance. That night, 114 people died when two of the hotel's "skybridges" collapsed, trapping hundreds of people under the debris. The photograph shows the one "skybidge" that did not fall, at the upper left.

LEFT: Outside the Hyatt Regency Hotel, medics administered first aid to the injured. Twenty-five ambulances, a helicopter, and dozens of privately owned vehicles were used to carry the injured to nearby hospitals.

RIGHT: A wider view of the damage to the dance floor and of the rescue operation.

people trapped underneath the debris had been crushed to death. Others had suffered only broken arms or legs. Twenty-five ambulances, a helicopter, and dozens of privately owned cabs, cars, and vans ferried the injured to nearby hospitals.

All through the night, rescuers continued the search for survivors. Each time they found one, cheers rang through the ruined space. At 6.00 a.m., the last ten survivors were found. An hour and a half hour later, workers lifted the last section of the skybridge, hoping to find at least one person still alive. Instead, they found thirty-one bodies, bringing the total number of fatalities to 114.

Workers set up a temporary morgue in the hotel's exhibition center. Slowing the progress of survivors into the morgue to identify bodies were puddles of water standing in the lobby. When the skybridges collapsed, they broke pipes which gushed water onto the wreckage. As work progressed, the water became tinged with blood.

Immediately after the disaster, the National Bureau of Standards put samples of the skybridges through rigorous tests. Officials at the federal agency declared that the materials themselves were sound. The problem lay with the design of the structure, and especially with a change made to the original design during construction.

As originally designed, each of the skybridges would have hung from hangar rods from the ceiling. During construction, however, the design was changed. Instead of hanging the bridges individually, the lower bridge was hung from the higher one. As a result, the load carried by the hangar rods was doubled. Although the new design was approved by the architects and engineers in charge of the project, they did not notifiy the city codes department of the change. The National Bureau of Standards found, too, that even the original design, which had been approved by the codes inspectors, did not comply with the standards set out by the city.

A Kansas City structural engineer on the scene shortly after the collapse noticed that some of the hangar rods still had small washers and nuts on their ends. He suggested that the small size of washers and nuts used was not sufficient to support the weight of the skybridges.

The victims' families and the injured survivors filed more than three billion dollars in lawsuits. Defendants included the Hyatt Hotels Corporation, the Crown Center Redevelopment Corporation, and architects, engineers, and contractors involved in the skybridges' design and construction. By October 1982, twenty-nine million dollars had been paid in out-of-court settlements to the plaintiffs.

Two and a half months after the tragic night of July 17, the Hyatt Regency reopened following a five-million-dollar renovation. Where the skybridges had once soared overhead, there was a new balcony supported by ten huge columns made of reinforced concrete and anchored firmly to bedrock.

ABOVE: The wreckage at the site of the Harbor Cay Condominium collapse in March 1981. The architect, two engineers, and two contractors were charged with negligence after the disaster.

RIGHT: Rescue workers carefully broke apart the top layer of concrete at the ruined Harbor Cay Condominium so that cranes could remove the fragments.

RIGHT: Fifty-one workers fell to their deaths from scaffolding on the uncompleted cooling tower at Willow Island, West Virginia, nuclear power plant on April 27, 1978.

ABOVE: The top and bottom of the cooling tower at Willow Island taken using a wide-angle lens. The wrecked scaffolding lies on the ground.

BELOW: Investigators searching for clues as to why the scaffolding collapsed at the Willow Island nuclear power plant.

CHAPTER SIX

EARTHQUAKES AND VOLCANOES

Mysteries abound just beneath the earth's surface. Although we cannot see it happen, the gargantuan plates on which the ground rests shift in opposite directions. Underground gases build up pressure, forcing huge mountains to form over millions of years. Most of the time, such geologic occurrences have little effect on the day-to-day lives of humans. Sometimes, however, nature goes wild. Volcanoes that have lain dormant for centuries suddenly spew forth ash and molten rock, destroying everything in their path. Geologic plates suddenly jerk apart, ripping open giant chasms in the earth.

RIGHT: Army troops patrolled the streets and worked with firemen to control the fires that followed the 1906 San Franciso earthquake. The army was also in charge of controlling looters, and had killed nearly a hundred citizens by the end of the disaster.

THE SAN FRANCISCO EARTHQUAKE 1906

At 5.12 a.m. on April 18, 1906, the area around San Francisco suffered a huge earthquake. Ancient redwoods toppled over, huge sections of the rocky shoreline collapsed into the sea, and San Francisco was in flames almost immediately, the fires caused by broken gas lines and stove fires in demolished buildings.

San Francisco's location had brought great wealth to the city. Situated on a fifty-mile-long peninsula jutting into the Pacific Ocean and bordered to the east by a large bay, the city's shoreline was a jumble of docks, wharves, and warehouses where shipping industries both received and shipped out valuable cargoes daily. However, the city's location also made it a precarious place to live. At the nearby San Andreas Fault, two geologic plates meet in an 800-mile-long line that runs almost parallel to the coast of California. The North American plate moves to the southeast and the Pacific plate pushes northwest at the rate of about two inches per year, normally without having any great effect on the coastline. At some points along the fault, however, the edges of the plates have been wedged into position for years. When the pressure finally builds up to such a point that the locked edges of the plates suddenly shift, an earthquake occurs. On the morning of April 18, the two plates suddenly jerked apart under the Pacific Ocean. Immediately, shock waves rushed toward the Californian coastline at about 7,000 miles an hour. The rip hit land at Point Arena, ninety miles north of San Francisco.

Like Chicago in 1871, San Francisco was a city of wood. All over Russian, Nob, and Telegraph Hills, wooden houses lined the streets. The wealthy neighborhood between Powell and Van Ness Avenues and the poor section of Chinatown were the same, and both mansions and shanties were soon fuel for fires. Within minutes of the quake, fifty fires were reported throughout the city. San Franciscans raced about the streets, which were filled with unusal noises: nails ripping out of the wood of collapsing buildings, church bells ringing wildly, gas hissing from broken lines, and water gushing from pipes.

At 6.15 a.m., Brigadier General Frederick Funston, commander of the Presidio, put the city under military control. He swiftly ordered out all troops to help the city's firemen and police and, at about 7.00 a.m., army troops marched into the city. Shortly after the troops

RIGHT: The scene of devastation in San Francisco after the 1906 earthquake, when damage to buildings was exacerbated by fires breaking out within minutes of the quake.

LEFT: While a stone building crumbled to the ground during the earthquake of 1906, its neighbor, a partially completed steel structure, remained intact.

BELOW: A view of Market Street, looking west from the Ferry Tower.

arrived, Mayor Eugene Schmitz, Jeremiah Dinan, the chief of police, and John Dougherty, who headed up the fire department after the chief was fatally injured in the quake, devised a plan to control the fires, but this was based on old information. They wanted to hold the fire in a line south of Market Street, but fire was already raging through the produce market to the north.

Firemen used dynamite to flatten buildings in the path of the fire in hopes of keeping the latter in check. Unfortunately, the dynamited buildings just went up in flames every time, and the sparks from the explosions flew through the air to ignite more buildings. Within six hours of the quake, the fire had spread up California Street.

Before noon, a new fire had started in Hayes Valley. Called the "ham-and-eggs" fire, it was started by a housewife lighting her kitchen stove. The earthquake had damaged the stove's flue, and sparks escaped from it all over the house. Within minutes, the ensuing fire jumped over Van Ness Avenue, raged up Larkin Street, and attacked the ruins of City Hall.

That same afternoon, Mayor Schmitz created volunteer committees for safety. These were charged with various aspects of disaster management. One of these was designed to hold profiteering at bay by arresting, for example, any draymen who took advantage of the circumstances to raise their rates for hauling household goods. Another of these was to ensure that saloonkeepers were obeying the mayor's order to close their businesses. Yet another was to patrol the streets to make certain that residents were following the mayor's prohibition on indoor cooking.

The New York Times.

"All the News That's Fit to Print."

THE WEATHER.
Fair to-day and to-morrow; rising southerly winds.

VOL. LV...NO. 17,617. ••••   NEW YORK, THURSDAY, APRIL 19, 1906.—TWENTY TWO PAGES.   ONE CENT In Greater New York, Jersey City and Newark. | Elsewhere, TWO CENTS

OVER 500 DEAD, $200,000,000 LOST IN SAN FRANCISCO EARTHQUAKE

Nearly Half the City Is in Ruins and 50,000 Are Homeless.

WATER SUPPLY FAILS AND DYNAMITE IS USED IN VAIN

Great Buildings Consumed Before Helpless Firemen—Federal Troops and Militia Guard the City, With Orders to Shoot Down Thieves—Citizens Roused in Early Morning by Great Convulsion and Hundreds Caught by Falling Walls.

ALL SAN FRANCISCO MAY BURN; CLIFF HOUSE RESORT IN SEA

Flames Carried From the Business Quarter to Residences

PALACE HOTEL AND MINT GO; BIG BUILDINGS BLOWN UP.

Other Shocks Felt During the Afternoon—Insane Asylum Is Wrecked and Hundreds of Former Inmates Are Roaming About the Country—Reports of Heavy Loss of Life at San Jose.

THE BUILDINGS DESTROYED.

EARTHQUAKE'S AUTOGRAPH AS IT WROTE IT 3,000 MILES AWAY.

Tracing Made by the Seismograph Needle in the Office of State Geologist John M. Clarke, State Museum, Albany, Showing How the Earthquake Traveled Across Continent in 19 Minutes.

LEFT: The April 19, 1906, edition of *The New York Times* devoted its entire front page to coverage of the San Francisco disaster.

RIGHT: Street damage caused by the 1906 earthquake in San Francisco.

BELOW: A view of Market Street, east from 6th Street, after the 1906 earthquake.

The troops continued blowing up buildings, despite the fact that, with each building they dynamited, new fires were started by flying sparks and debris. The army was successful, though, in its watch for looters. Early that afternoon and without permission from the city officials, Brigadier General Funston ordered his troops to shoot looters. After several city residents had been executed, without warning claim some authorities, the mayor agreed to post a warning. Unconstitutional as it was, it stated that the federal troops and the police force had been "authorized to KILL any and all persons found engaged in Looting or in the Commission of Any Other Crime." By the end of the disaster, up to a hundred San Francisco residents had been killed by the army troops.

When evening came, the fire still raged unchecked. Troops now blew up the drugstore at Clay and Kearney Streets with black powder, and the force hurled debris across the street into Chinatown. Most of Chinatown's residents had evacuated the area earlier in the day, but still there was a menace of particular concern: tens of

thousands of rats. When the troops entered Chinatown and started blowing up buildings, the rats, long known to be carriers of bubonic plague, fled from their burning homes into the rest of the city. The danger to public health was immense.

By 8.00 p.m. that evening, the fire covered three square miles of San Francisco. It destroyed the Post Office, the grand Palace Hotel, the offices of *The Daily News*, *The Examiner*, *Call*, and *Chronicle*, and the Grand Opera House, where perhaps the most famous visitor to San Francisco that day, Enrico Caruso, had starred in *Carmen* the night before. The city's libraries, the Mercantile, Bohemian Club, Pioneer, French, German, B'nai B'rith, and Law Libraries, were also devoured along with more than a million books.

The first relief arrived in San Francisco at midnight, while the city was still in flames. A train loaded with doctors, nurses, food, and medical supplies pulled in from Los Angeles nineteen hours after the earthquake. In New York, William Randolph Hearst urged readers of his newspapers to donate their spare change to the relief effort, and less than twenty-four hours after the quake, he sent twelve trains loaded with supplies across the country. The Southern Pacific Railroad provided free transportation to refugees and established a refugee center at the Oakland train station.

In the early hours of April 19, the Barbary Coast went up in flames. An area of brothels, dance halls, pawn-shops, and saloons, all fitted with wooden tables and benches and with sawdust on the floors, it had no chance of escaping the inferno. The Fairmont Hotel caught fire that morning, too, and the mayor and his disaster committee were forced to find new headquarters.

With the flames advancing on Van Ness Avenue, the army decided to blow up all the houses on the south side of the street, creating a trench fifty yards wide. The troops ordered residents to evacuate the area, giving them little time to gather up possessions. When the dynamite was set off, a stretch of Van Ness Avenue almost a mile long lay in ruins. On Friday, the fire came close to the north side of Van Ness, but suddenly the wind shifted, blowing the blaze back on itself.

The last section of San Francisco still burning was the waterfront area. Army troops and firemen, exhausted by three days of firefighting, finally brought the blaze under control at 7.15 a.m. on Saturday, April 21.

The extent of the destruction was enormous. Almost five square miles had been consumed by the fire and 28,000 buildings had been destroyed. Estimates of

LEFT: Residents of San Francisco preparing a meal outdoors. Thousands of San Franciscans were left homeless after the 1906 earthquake, and even those whose homes were undamaged were forbidden from cooking indoors by order of the mayor.

damage to property ranged from 350 to 500 million dollars. Throughout the country, insurance companies went bankrupt attempting to meet their liabilities. Only six insurance companies paid claims in full. In all, about eighty percent of the value of insured property was covered by insurance companies. San Franciscans received nine million dollars in relief funds, including 45,000 dollars from the Empress of China and 245,000 dollars from the Japanese Red Cross.

The official count released by the city was 478 dead. In a new work by Gladys Hanson and Emmet Condon, the fatality figures are much higher. After years of research, they state in *Denial of Disaster* that more than 3,000 people died in the earthquake and ensuing fire. In addition, they present overwhelming evidence of photographs having been retouched before their submission to insurance companies as claims. Desperate to receive compensation for their losses, San Franciscans tried to prove that their homes and business establishments had remained intact through the earthquake, a disaster against which they were not insured, only to be consumed by the fire, for which they could make claims.

ABOVE: The ruined city of San Francisco and its homeless citizens after the earthquake and fire.

LEFT: San Franciscans in their new outdoor home after the 1906 earthquake.

RIGHT: A view of Market Street from McAllister.

TOP LEFT: A block of Howard Street at 17th Street with damaged houses. The houses that were located in the foreground of the photograph were destroyed by fire.

RIGHT: Observers gathered on Russian Hill to watch the fires raging through the city. To stop the spread of fire, Army troops and firemen dynamited buildings to form firebreaks. Often, however, they succeeded only in lighting new fires.

BELOW LEFT: Mason Street at 6:25 a.m. on the morning of April 18, 1906, with fires raging in the background.

THE ALASKA EARTHQUAKE 1964

About 150 miles southeast of Anchorage, Alaska, deep in the waters of Prince William Sound, the rocks bordering the Fairweather Fault suddenly shifted at 5.36 p.m. on March 27, 1964. This shift sent shock waves toward Alaska's shoreline at thousands of miles an hour. Within minutes on that Good Friday afternoon, 118 Alaskans were dead and 4,500 were left homeless.

Seismologists measured the quake at between 8.4 and 8.6 on the Richter Scale, making it the largest quake on record in America. The shocks were felt as far away as Houston, Texas. Residents of South Africa reported seeing the water in their wells sloshing about. Closer to the epicenter a tidal wave demolished four square blocks and killed ten people in Crescent City, California.

The damage in Alaska was enormous and totaled more than 500 million dollars' worth. In Anchorage, people rushed into the streets, trying to flee from the buildings that were crashing down everywhere. In the streets, they faced another danger. The pavement had broken into huge chunks, which sank into the ground. Street signs, building facades, and people slid into the gaping chasms. People held on to whatever seemed stable. More than a hundred people, including one man who had run naked from a sauna, joined hands in a long chain, desperately trying to stay away from the splits in the earth. Two of the chasms measured twelve feet deep and fifty feet wide. In all, a thirty-block section of Alaska's largest city was destroyed.

In Kodiak, a seventeen-foot tsunami, or tidal wave, swept over the harbor docks and into the downtown section. Some of the boats harbored at Kodiak landed several blocks from the shore. Others were smashed to smithereens. Two canneries, so important to the city's economy, were washed away in the waves.

In Seward, the town burst into flames as oil-storage tanks ruptured. Seward was an important year-round port, and warehouses and piers had been built along its silty shoreline. When the tidal wave hit the harbor, the pilings supporting the waterfront buildings collapsed. Standard Oil Company's eight storage tanks spilled thousands of gallons of oil and gasoline into the water. Texaco's eight tanks exploded, and fire spread out over the land and the sea.

In Valdez, 125 miles east of Anchorage, a giant sea wave crashed into a 100-foot-long pier. The twenty-eight people who had been unloading the *Chena* fell into the water, and were all washed out to sea. Three quarters of the downtown area was under water.

President Lyndon B. Johnson declared Alaska a national disaster area. Within days, money poured in from all over the country. Repairing the damage would

BELOW: An aerial view of earthquake damage along Cook Inlet near Anchorage, Alaska. The epicenter of the 1964 earthquake was about 150 miles southeast of Anchorage in Prince William Sound.

RIGHT: A 7,000-gallon cement storage tank toppled over when the earthquake struck the city of Anchorage.

BELOW: One of many bridges along the Anchorage-Seward highway destroyed in the earthquake. The state's economy was also devastated by the earthquake; three fourths of its businesses and industries were ruined.

need a lot of money, particularly as three quarters of Alaska's industries and businesses had been destroyed.

In a quake as large as this one, which was about double the force of the San Francisco earthquake of 1906, it is remarkable that no more than 118 people died. Working in favor of the Alaskans was the fact that schools and most businesses had already closed for the holiday weekend when the buildings that housed them tumbled to the ground. In addition, the thousands of tourists who normally flock to Alaska during the vacation season had not yet arrived. Fortunately, too, the weather was not as cold as it sometimes is in late March. The moderate temperature of 28°F kept those people caught outdoors from freezing to death.

BELOW: Anchorage's new J.C. Penney Co. store crumbled to the ground, killing two people, in the March 27, 1964, earthquake in Alaska. Property damage totaled more than $500 million and 118 people were killed in thequake that measured 8.4 to 8.6 on the Richter Scale.

RIGHT: A section of Fourth Avenue, the main thoroughfare in Anchorage, sank twenty feet below street level, taking a row of parked cars with it, during the March 1964 earthquake.

LEFT: Bulldozers begin clearing debris from Fourth Avenue in Anchorage, Alaska's largest city.

RIGHT AND BELOW: Aerial views of earthquake damage in Alaska, including damage near Kodiak, where a seventeen-foot tidal wave swept over the harbor docks and into the downtown section.

THE SAN FRANCISCO EARTHQUAKE 1989

For more than eighty years, San Franciscans put the memory of the great 1906 earthquake and fire behind them. Although tremors continued to rock the city periodically, no major disaster occurred again – until 1989. That year on October 17, as 58,000 fans packed the house at Candlestick Park to watch the World Series between the Oakland Athletics and the San Francisco Giants, an earthquake measuring 6.9 on the Richter scale rumbled through the area.

The quake struck at 5:04 p.m., during the rush hour, catching thousands of people in their cars as they headed for home. Along Interstate 880 in Oakland, a section of the upper level a mile and a quarter long plummeted down onto the lower roadway, killing dozens of people. Rescuers worked throughout the night and the following few days trying to free survivors pinned under the wreckage. Dogs were brought in to help in the search for survivors. When survivors were found, doctors were called in to treat their injuries while rescue workers tried to free the victims from the tangled mess. As much as eighty-nine hours after the earthquake, rescuers pulled another survivor, a fifty-seven-year-old union clerk, out of the wreckage.

A thirty-foot-long section of the San Francisco-Oakland Bay Bridge collapsed, and a few cars hung from the upper level of the bridge. In Union Square, the plate-glass windows of I.Magnin department store shattered, severely cutting pedestrians.

Throughout the city, water, electricity, telephone, and transportation systems were rendered useless. In the Marina district, several apartment buildings caught fire. When buildings in the area were still swaying days after the earthquake, the authorities razed some and allowed others to fall down of their own accord.

In Santa Cruz, fifteen miles south of the earthquake's epicenter, a shopping center, Pacific Garden Mall, also suffered heavy damage, and four people were killed.

Californians are in the habit of thinking about "the big one." The 1989 earthquake was not it. The next day, joggers were out on the streets, and families thronged to the city's parks on their unexpected holiday. After inspectors had examined buildings to ensure that they were safe for occupation, workers went back to their offices and children went back to school, and for most San Franciscans life returned to normal.

RIGHT: A fireman keeping watch over an apartment building that was destroyed in the San Francisco earthquake of 1989.

RIGHT: President George Bush toured the disaster area on October 20, 1989, three days after the earthquake.

RIGHT: On October 17, 1989, an earthquake measuring 6.9 on the Richter scale struck San Francisco, Oakland, and the nearby area. One section of Interstate Highway I80, which leads to the Bay Bridge, sustained massive damage, and several people were crushed in their cars.

ABOVE: Rescue workers pulling a car from the lower level of the Bay Bridge, where it fell during the 1989 San Francisco earthquake.

LEFT: The thirty-foot section of the Bay Bridge that collapsed during the 1989 earthquake, trapping motorists on the lower level.

RIGHT: San Francisco's Marina District went up in flames after the 1989 earthquake struck the city.

RIGHT: Power was out all over San Francisco the night of the 1989 earthquake, and many residents spent the night in tents erected in the parks.

MOUNT ST. HELENS 1981

The countryside around Washington State's Mount St. Helen's was like a picture postcard. Rising out of dense forests traversed by beautiful trout streams, Mount St. Helens, some 9,667 feet high, looked like a perfectly symmetrical dome. For more than a century, the volcanic mountain had remained dormant – just another sleeping giant in the Cascade Mountain Range that stretches from northern California to British Columbia. Sports fishermen and nature lovers flocked to the area, which abounded with fish and other wildlife. Then one day, all that ended. The eruption of Mount St. Helens wiped out the native blacktailed deer, mountain lions, elk, Chanook salmon, and steelhead trout in a matter of moments. In its fury, it also killed at least sixty-two people.

The eruption of Mount St. Helens on May 18, 1981, was not without warnings. Almost two months earlier, the area had been plagued with hundreds of earthquake tremors, sometimes as many as forty an hour. On March 27, the mountainside erupted, shooting steam and hot ash 6,500 feet into the air. This relatively small eruption created a new crater 220 feet across, which continued to emit ominous rumbling noises from its center.

RIGHT: On May 18, 1981, Mount St. Helens, in Washington, erupted with tremendous fury. The entire northern face of the volcanic mountain slid down into Spirit Lake and Toutle River. Sixty-two people were killed, and the entire populations of blacktail deer, mountain lions, elk, chinook salmon, and steelhead trout were annihilated.

LEFT: A five-foot-high ridge of volcanic mud covered the mailboxes at the Camelot Trailer Court in Castle Rock, Washington, after the 1981 Mount St. Helens eruption. Bill Pfeifer, a resident of the trailer court, had to bend down to check his mailbox.

The United States Geological Center set up a volcano watch using nearby Vancouver as its headquarters. Almost everyday, a scientist or two would make the trip to the mountain to install special monitoring equipment, such as seismographs, tiltmeters, and thermal gauges. Sightseers, too, came to the mountain, hoping to witness the eruption that seemed imminent.

The scientists and sightseers did not have long to wait before the mountain started changing before their eyes. The bulge on the side started to expand, at the rate of nearly five feet every day, to a total projection of 300 feet. Something big was clearly about to happen.

Governor Dixy Lee Ray ordered the area within a five-mile radius of the mountain top to be evacuated and all roads leading to the mountain were blocked to keep sightseers away. As things turned out, this evacuation order proved to be very necessary, but should have encompassed a larger area.

On May 18, 1981, at 8.32 a.m., Mount St. Helens erupted again, and this time the damage was severe. All at once the north slope of the mountain, where the bulge had been growing, slid off into Spirit Lake and Toutle River. Then the underground gases and ground water, which had changed to steam, forced their way horizontally through what was left of the northern slope. Through this vent, another eruption shot straight up, sending smoke and ash twelve miles into the sky.

The first eruption, the horizontal one, and the debris from the avalanche rushed forward at 250 miles an hour. Traveling seventeen miles north and covering 200 square miles, the molten rock and mountain fragments knocked down everything in their path. Scientists found later that six million mature trees had fallen in the path of the volcanic material. They also assumed that some of the sixty-two people who were killed in the disaster were mowed down by the trees or swept away in the lava. Most of the dead, however, had been suffocated by the ash flying through the air.

It is difficult to imagine the fury of the eruption and the force of the landslide. Boiling mud swirled everywhere at tremendous speeds. Nothing in its path was safe. A mobile home parked eleven miles north of

BELOW: A crewman aboard an army helicopter surveying the damage caused by the eruption of Mount St. Helens in May 1981. A count confirmed that six million mature trees had been felled in the path of the volcanic matter.

the mountain was thrown 600 feet. Thirteen miles from the mountain, a truck's plastic components turned to liquid. Fishermen on the Green River, sixteen miles away, were burned by searing debris. The mudflow crashed into a ridge across Spirit Lake and then spread out through the Toutle River valley. As it cooled, it formed a mile-wide lumpy ridge some thirteen miles long and hundreds of feet high. Pushed from its normal course, the Toutle River reached record high levels. The Cowlitz River was clogged with volcanic debris, and the Columbia River, normally forty feet deep in the middle of its navigation channel, was no longer deep enough for the seagoing vessels harbored at Portland.

People as far away as western Montana were blanketed with volcanic fallout. In Yakima, eighty-five miles east of the mountain, the sky turned black at noon on the day of the big eruption. In late May, two new eruptions sent up more ash, which was borne westward by the wind, covering northwestern Oregon and the rest of Washington State. Apple growers were forced to hose forced air or water onto their trees in order to save their harvests. City dwellers suffered through traffic clogged by stalled cars.

Despite all this damage, it seemed that the mountain had still not spent its fury, and it continued to erupt until September. The U.S. Army Corps of Engineers went to work immediately. Fearing that heavy spring rains would flood the area clogged by volcanic debris, the corps built dams to help control the water and dredged out river channels for months. Within six months, the Cowlitz, Columbia, and Toutle Rivers had been freed from 100 million cubic yards of volcanic debris. The dredging alone cost 250 million dollars.

Surrounding Mount St. Helens today is a public park spreading out over 100,000 acres. Amazingly, nature is renewing itself in the devasted area. New populations of elk have made their way to the preserve. Native vegetation, such as fireweed, upright huckleberries, and everlasting lupine grow abundantly. In fact, within only three years of the eruption, ninety percent of the plant species that had originally thrived in the area had reestablished themselves.

BELOW: The mountain continued sporadically to spew out smoke, ash, and molten rock for several months. The eruption pictured here, which shot smoke and ash 45,000 feet into the air, occurred on March 20, 1982.

CHAPTER SEVEN

INDUSTRIAL AND MINING

Year after year, the Occupational Safety and Health Administration issues new standards to make Americans' places of employment safe. Inspectors check office buildings annually to ensure that employees can safely evacuate their spaces in the event of fire. The Nuclear Regulatory Commission examines nuclear power plants to ensure not only that the general public is safe but also that power plant workers are not being exposed to deadly radiation. Yet, despite the efforts of federal, state, and local inspectors, accidents do happen.

In the deadliest of all industrial accidents, a Union Carbide plant leaked a toxic gas called methyl isocyanate into the atmosphere at Bhopal, in India, on December 3 1984, killing 2,500 and injuring 200,000. Then, on August 11, 1985, the company's plant in Institute, West Virginia, started leaking aldicarb oxime, a chemical that is mixed with methyl isocyanate to make a pesticide. Thirty-six minutes after the company discovered the leaking tank, it sounded an alarm, by which time 135 people had been sickened by the fumes. Union Carbide came under attack for not warning the public of the danger earlier. A company spokesmen said that a computer in the plant had predicted that the toxic fumes would not spread to the surrounding town but would stay within the plant's grounds. Nevertheless, spread they did, and throughout the town people sought treatment for eye irritation, burning sensations in their throats, and vomiting.

The most famous recent industrial accident in America was that at Three Mile Island. It was here that, at 4.00 a.m. on March 28, 1979, the turbine driven by steam created by the nuclear reactor suddenly shut down. At first the engineers in charge thought the malfunction was due to a faulty pump. Then, at about 6.00 a.m., they noticed that water had seeped onto the floor of the containment building. This told them that the loop that brought water to the reactor core in order to keep it at a safe 600°F had somehow been damaged. In spite of Metropolitan Edison's public relations statements to the contrary, a nuclear meltdown, or "China syndrome," was perilously close.

Less well known, but more deadly, than Union Carbide's plant leak in Institute, West Virginia, or Three Mile Island's close brush with a meltdown are the three accidents presented below.

RIGHT: Security guards keeping their posts at the gates of the Three Mile Island nuclear power plant after the March 28, 1979, leak of radioactive material.

The Triangle Shirtwaist Fire, New York City 1911

On Saturday morning, March 25, 1911, 500 employees, mostly young women, reported for work at the Triangle Shirtwaist factory in New York City. Located in the top three floors of the ten-story Asch Building, at Greene Street and Washington Place, the factory was to become a death trap for all those inside that day.

The Asch Building had been built in 1901. At the time of its construction, it met the requirements of the few fire laws on the books and had been proclaimed "fireproof." The existing laws only required stone floors and metal window frames to be fitted in buildings of eleven floors or more, so the ten-story Asch Building, with its wooden floors and window trim, met this requirement.

New York City's fire department knew that the law needed to be changed. The fire chief told the city time and again that equipment could only reach only the seventh floor of any building. In comparison with modern-day safety standards, it seems remarkable that the Asch Building was considered fireproof. Inside, workers were jammed tightly together. The building only satisfied the requirement that each worker have 250 cubic feet of air around him or her because of its extremely high ceilings. Workers sat on wooden chairs at wooden tables. Oil from their sewing machines dripped onto the floor. Everywhere one looked there were heaps of fabric destined to become fashionable shirtwaists, or high-necked, full-sleeved blouses.

When the bell signaling the end of work rang on the afternoon of March 25, one of the young women preparing to leave her eighth-floor work station noticed that a rag bin under a cutting table was on fire. Some of the cutters immediately sprang into action immediately to try and extinguish the blaze, but the fire quickly spread to pattern pieces hanging over the table. All around piles of fabric began to burn, and the room filled with smoke.

Superintendent Samuel Bernstein called out for someone to bring the fire hose, but as workers reached for it, they discovered it had rotted. These Triangle employees now had three means of escape. They could use the freight elevators, the fire escape, or the stairways.

The fire escape, a steep, ladder-like structure, only reached to the second floor, stopping short above the courtyard. Climbing down the escape, several young women fell from one landing to the next. One man fell all the way from the eighth floor to the courtyard.

LEFT: The Asch Building, New York City, where, on March 25, 1911, a fire broke out on the eighth floor. Workers on the eighth, ninth, and tenth floors, all employees of the Triangle Shirtwaist Factory, desperately tried to escape the inferno. Built in 1901, the building was "fireproof" by the standards of the time.

ABOVE RIGHT: The managers of the Triangle Shirtwaist Factory locked the doors to the stairways each day for security reasons. On the day of the fire, the young women tried desperately to smash open the door pictured here so that they could escape.

RIGHT: When the fire broke out, some employees operated the elevator in an attempt to carry the 500 employees of the Triangle Shirtwaist Factory to safety. Some employees jumped onto car as it descended, eventually crushing the top of the elevator unit.

BELOW: A net was stretched for the Triangle Shirtwaist Factory employees to jump into, but often they jumped in pairs, ripping through the net. Outside the building, bodies lay in the street.

The staircases were not much better. Workers on the eighth floor rushed to the staircase on the Washington Place side of the building, but the door to the stairway was locked. Rushing to yet another staircase, they found it clogged with workers trying to flee from the ninth and tenth floors. The freight elevator was now their only hope, and several times the cutters ran the elevator up and down loaded with terrified employees.

On the tenth floor, about seventy people were preparing to leave work when the fire broke out two floors below them. Many of these workers fled onto the roof where they were aided by students of New York University, whose building was situated across the street. The ingenious students stretched ladders that had been left in the building by painters across the street to the Asch Building, and one by one the workers crept across the makeshift bridge to safety. Only one person from the tenth floor died that day, and she panicked and jumped out a window, on hearing news of the fire.

On the ninth floor, 260 people had work stations at eight tables lined on either side with sewing machines. The tables were butted up against the Washington Place wall, so that there was only one entrance and exit to each row. Workers did not know that a fire of deadly magnitude was raging one floor below them until it was too late for them to evacuate the building. The eighth-floor workers had telephoned a warning up to the ninth and tenth floors, but for some reason, the telephone on the ninth floor did not ring.

About a hundred people managed to squeeze safely down the narrow staircase to the Greene Street exit. With the Washington Street staircase locked, there were only the fire escape and the freight elevator left. Overloaded with hundreds of people, the fire escape broke away from the wall and shattered to the ground. Bodies littered the courtyard. The freight elevator was already loaded with people from the eighth and tenth floors. Some ninth-floor employees grabbed hold of the elevator cables and lowered themselves down. Others jumped down the shaft landing on top of the elevator car, which soon caved in from the excess weight.

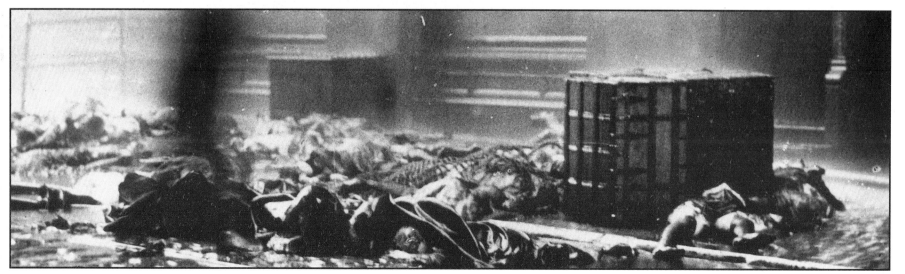

The remaining people on the ninth floor raced to the windows, which were about 100 feet above the pavement. Firemen had stretched out a net to catch the jumpers but, in their panic, the young women jumped in pairs or in threes, ripping through the net and rendering it useless.

Thirty-five pieces of firefighting equipment responded to the alarm. Both horse-drawn and motorized equipment came to the scene, but were of little help. Standing on the ledge of the ninth floor, the young women watched hopefully as the Hook and Ladder

Company Twenty raised its ladder toward them. It was too short; it only reached the sixth floor.

Outside on the street, a huge crowd had gathered. Within fifteen minutes of the fire's start, 10,000 people watched in dismay as the building burned and scores of young women jumped to their deaths.

A temporary morgue was created on 26th Street, and huge crowds of survivors waited in lines to enter the building and identify the bodies of their friends and relatives. Seven bodies were never identified. On April 5, the city buried the unknown victims, and the Women's

BELOW: Crowds of people gathered at the foot of the 26th Street pier to enter a temporary morgue, which held the bodies of victims of the fire at the Triangle Shirtwaist Factory.

RIGHT: The ruins of the Triangle Shirtwaist Factory. Before the fire, the space held rows of tables at which sewing machine operators and cutters worked. Piles of fabric lay everywhere, and oil from sewing machines dripped on the floor. The fire broke out in a rag bin under a cutting table.

BELOW: The families of victims search the morgue for loved ones who died in the Triangle Shirtwaist Factory fire.

Trade Union League and the International Ladies' Garment Workers Union led a parade in memory of the 146 people who had died.

Three months after the fire, the New York Factory Investigating Commission was established. Mandated to examine the working conditions in factories throughout the state, the commission worked for two and a half years. Members of the commission included Samuel Gompers, founder of the American Federation of Labor, and Mary E. Dreier, president of the Women's Trade Union League. The commission's report caused sweeping changes to be made in New Yorkers' places of employment.

The 146 workers who died in the Triangle factory fire are honored by a plaque on a New York University building that now occupies the site of the old Asch Building. "Out of their martyrdom," it reads, "came new concepts of social responsibility and labor legislation that had helped make American working conditions the finest in the world."

THE CENTRALIA, PENNSYLVANIA, MINE FIRE 1981

No single date can be placed on the Centralia Mine Fire. When the fire broke out in 1962, John F. Kennedy was president and had stirred the nation two years earlier by saying, "Ask not what your country can do for you. Ask what you can do for your country." In 1981 during a protest march, residents of Centralia carried signs that read, "Ask not what your country can do for you – it doesn't give a damn." A review of the events during the intervening nineteen years would persuade even the most idealistic government supporter of the truth of the placard's statement. Although no deaths can be linked directly to the fire, the period of time the disaster spanned was enormous, stretching from 1962 to 1985, when New Centralia became home to many of the refugees from Centralia.

In 1962, the Council of Centralia, a coal-mining town in the Appalachian Mountains, faced a problem that plagues city governments everywhere – where to locate a new landfill. After a great deal of debate, the council members settled on a site near St. Ignatius Cemetery. The site was approved by the regional landfill inspector after the city sealed several mine openings that had been uncovered during strip mining. In May of that year, the council wanted the landfill cleaned up before the Memorial Day holiday weekend. The only record of what happened next is in the council minutes, which contain bills submitted by five firemen for putting out a fire in the landfill. A few days later, residents of Centralia noticed more flames. The firemen returned to the site on June 4 and hosed it down from about 9.00 p.m. until 2.00 a.m. Again the fire rekindled itself, and while at work at the site, the firemen discovered a hole in the landfill that led down into the old underground mine shafts. In mid-July, when George Segaritus made an inspection visit to the Centralia landfill, he noticed steam wisping out of the hole. A state mine inspector called in to examine the hole confirmed Segaritus's fears: the old mines below the landfill were on fire.

Centralia's city council requested help from the state's Department of Mines and Mineral Industries (DMMI) in putting out the fire and waited to receive word about the type of assistance they could expect. The fire, however, did not wait. It crept along the underground labyrinth of mine shafts and tunnels, in which temperatures reached 1,000°F. Oxygen from open mine shafts and from the drain tunnel that ended at Big Mine Run a mile east of Centralia fed the flames.

Mine fires are not unusual occurrences. Sometimes they start when gas explodes deep in the mine's interior.

LEFT: A U.S. Bureau of Mines employee checked the temperature regularly at various boreholes placed throughout Centralia. The reading at this site was 720 degrees in November 1979. None of the efforts to control the fire was sufficiently funded to accomplish the job.

Sometimes lanterns brought in to illuminate the work area tip their combustible contents onto the mine floor. Although not unusual, mine fires are particularly difficult to control. One company, the Lehigh Navigation Coal Company, waged a two-million-dollar battle aginst a fire in one of its mines for more than eighty years.

State mine inspectors converged on Centralia in August 1962. What they discovered called for drastic action. They ordered all the mines around Centralia to be closed. Deputy Secretary of Mines James Shober recommended to his department that the state should pay for extinguishing the fire, a job that entailed digging out the burning area at a cost of approximately 30,000 dollars. On August 17, the state awarded a contract to dig out the area to Bridy, Inc.. The company went to work on August 22, but by October 29, when all the allocated money had been spent, the fire was still raging.

The next operation was mounted in November by K&H Evcavating. The state hired the company to fill the burning mine with a mixture of crushed rock and water, in order to suffocate the flames. By mid-December, state officials knew that this project would fail. Drilling holes had been placed too close to the fire area, and water was in short supply due to the abnormally severe winter weather, which froze water lines.

BELOW: The mine fire in Centralia, Pennsylvania, started in 1962, and raged out of control for more than twenty years. Residents of the town were caught in a seemingly endless tangle of red tape in their attempts to get help to extinguish the fire. By 1981, when this photograph was taken, gas was still escaping from vents placed in the mine tunnels.

When the K&H project ended in March and the fire was still out of control, and H. Beecher Charmbury, secretary of mines for Pennsylvania, allocated another 40,000 dollars for a new effort in Centralia. The state agency then asked the Federal Bureau of Mines to contribute funds to the project, matching those funds allocated by the state. The bureau replied that it had no further funds available for such projects and that Pennsylvania would have to wait until the beginning of the new fiscal year, October 1, 1963, for any federal assistance. With only 40,000 dollars available, Gordon Smith, the deputy secretary of mines, decided to dig a trench to cut off the fire in the mine gangway and prevent its movement to the east. In October, workers digging the trench found that the fire had not been contained to the west of the excavation. It was now on both sides of the trench. The third project had failed, and no further efforts would be made to extinguish the fire for three and a half years.

In 1965, President Lyndon Baines Johnson's administration cut the political red tape that had plagued attempts to control the Centralia mine fire from its beginning. The Appalachian Regional Development Act put huge sums of money at the disposal of states in the mountain region to help these impoverished areas. Cleaning up old mine sites and extinguishing mine fires were projects that could be carried out with the funds allocated by the act. The federal government would pay for seventy-five percent of the cost of fighting mine fires; the state would pick up the other twenty-five percent.

Centralia then came under the bureaucratically minded control of Charles Kuebler, chief of the U.S. Bureau of Mines office in Wilkes-Barre. Kuebler designed a huge, three-phase project for Centralia, which would cost an estimated two and a half million dollars. Early on in the project, a trench was to be dug around the boundary of the fire. Because the proposed trench would cross private property, releases were needed from property owners. Kuebler's office spent an entire year gathering these releases; meanwhile, the fire was spreading. When the first exploratory drilling was done to determine the extent of the fire, workers found that it had spread under the homes on Centralia's Park Street, Locust Avenue, and Wood Street. The plans were now reworked. Kuebler decided to abandon the trench and build flush barriers instead, even though it was known among Bureau of Mine officials that such barriers provided only a temporary check to mine fires.

In December 1967, state inspectors discovered carbon monoxide in a house on Park Street. In a subsequent inspection, the gas could no longer be detected, and state officials declared that the cause of the gas in the home had been a faulty furnace. All along Park Street, Locust Avenue, and Wood Street, however, residents were suffering from several unexplained illnesses. Headaches, nausea, and drowsiness were common complaints yet, whenever residents left their houses and breathed the fresh air outdoors, the symptoms subsided. Some residents began to notice that their houseplants were dying.

The Bureau of Mines in the Nixon administration was headed by John O'Leary. New plans for Centralia called for a trench of much smaller proportions than the one in Kuebler's 1967 proposal. All summer, workers dug the trench, uncovering the glowing coal. More money would be needed to dig out the fire completely, but both the state and federal agencies terminated the project in October. Backhoes began filling in the trench.

The government agencies assured the residents of Centralia that the fire was being controlled by the fly-ash barrier shot down into the mines. Some residents knew better, however. They diligently monitored the temperatures of drilling holes and found that, as the months passed, these temperatures were rising. Finally, on December 8, 1976, a story in *News-Item* reported that lethal gases were leaking from the burning mine into

houses in Centralia. Great activity followed, but no money was forthcoming.

In July 1977, the Bureau of Mines and the Department of Environmental Resources started a cooperative project in Centralia. First, the agencies commissioned new bore holes to redetermine the extent of the fire. Next, they repaired the leaky ash barrier by shooting more filler into the mine, to fill two pits that were venting the mine's gases into the atmosphere. Residents grew alarmed when the filling began. They knew that, without the pits, the gases would seek other ways of escape. The Bureau of Mines assured residents that no homes in Centralia would be affected by the backed-up gases, due to the seventy feet of bedrock between the surface of the ground and the mine. Residents were unconvinced. They demanded a new trench to excavate the fire.

The Appalachian Regional Commission funded the new trench, which did not pass through any homes. The Bureau of Mines decided, however, that an area around the trench should nevertheless be cleared for safety reasons. Some families agreed to be relocated; others firmly refused. Since the project would not begin for several months, the Bureau of Mines offered Centralia residents carbon monoxide detectors that they could install in their homes. Unfortunately, there were never enough to go round, and some families remained on the waiting list for detectors for years.

On November 21, 1979, John Coddington, owner of a gas station, noticed that steam was rising from a hole in a lot next to his station. State officials inspected the hole that day and found that the air above it was at 66°F and that no carbon monoxide was present. The next day, however, the temperature was 122°F. When inspectors first tested the gasoline tank at the station, the temperature was eight degrees above the normal 50°F. The next day, it had risen to 64°F. The state fire marshal had no choice. He ordered the station to be closed and the tank to be emptied of gasoline.

Meanwhile, residents continued to get sick. Especially vulnerable to the effects of carbon monoxide and carbon dioxide were children, pregnant women, and people with asthma and other respiratory diseases, such as black lung disease, which is common in every coal-mining town. Alarms from the carbon monoxide detectors scattered throughout the town sounded with increasing frequency, and in the winter of 1980, the children at St. Ignatius School began suffering from headaches.

In February 1981, an event that would create widespread alarm occurred when a delegation of politicians and government employees visited Centralia to meet with the city council and to tour the area. Midway through the tour, a twelve-year-old boy named Todd Domboski raced toward the group to report what had just happened to him. While running across his neighbors' backyards, he had spied smoke emerging from a small hole in the ground. As he neared the hole, the ground suddenly sank. The more he fought to

escape, the more the ground gave way. Eric Wolfgang, Todd's sixteen-year-old cousin, had heard the boy's cries for help and miraculously managed to pull him to safety. Todd had been in the hole for about forty-five seconds. Hearing the boy's story, the officials touring Centralia sprang into action. One called Pennsylvania Governor Dick Thornburgh and pleaded with him to declare a state of emergency in the town. The governor declined, citing lack of necessary information.

Subsidence, or the caving in of old mine openings, continued sporadically in the town, yet federal and state money was still not made available to extinguish the fire. Governor Thornburgh visited Centralia on March 31, 1981, to announce the agreement the state had signed with the Department of the Interior. The agreement called for the federal government to purchase those homes within a sixteen-acre area and to relocate the families living there. Thornburgh edged around the question of who would extinguish the fire, saying only that the state would do all it could for the town. The state and the Department of the Interior were at a standoff, each waiting for the other to take responsibility for the problem, while residents continued to suffer from the potentially deadly fumes of the fire.

ABOVE: By November 1983, the situation along Highway 61 had worsened. The Department of Transportation was forced to close the road because of subsidence caused by Centralia's mine fire.

RIGHT: In January 1983, the surface of Highway 61 began to crack due to the intense heat from the Centralia mine fire. Department of Transportation employees measured the cracks in the road surface frequently.

In May 1982, state inspectors from the Department of Natural Resources discovered that carbon monoxide was entering Centralia's houses through sewer pipes. A few months later, lawyers working on behalf of the Concerned Citizens Action Group Against the Centralia Mine Fire announced to the city council that the group had legal grounds to sue the Office of Surface Mining within the Department of the Interior because after the office had relocated sixty-eight residents of Centralia, it had not taken any action to reclaim the land. Centralia residents split over the proposed lawsuit. The city council wanted no part of it. Many residents suspected that the city council was completely at the beck and call of Governor Thornburgh. Matters reached a head when *News-Item* broke the story that a bore hole had been discovered to have temperatures higher than 500°F and that the city council had not warned the townspeople of the situation.

The Office of Surface Mining commissioned a study of the situation in Centralia from GAI, Inc., a Pittsburgh geotechnical engineering company. On July 12, 1983, GAI released its report stating that, at that time, the fire encompassed 195 acres. To the horror of Centralia residents, GAI reported that the fire could eventually spread over 3,700 acres, encompassing all of Centralia, Brynesville, and the little village of Germantown. GAI recommended yet another trench to fight the fire. This trench was to be of mammoth proportions, measuring 3,700 feet long and 450 feet deep. Its optimum location was thought to be the middle of Centralia. Three other trenches would be needed around the town. The total cost would run to between 105 and 115 million dollars.

Centralia's city council studied the report carefully. They scheduled a referendum to determine whether the town should relocate at government expense or stay at its present site and hope money would be forthcoming to fight the fire. In the August 11 referendum, the vote was 345 to 200 in favor of relocation. Congressman Frank Harrison then attached to the Department of the Interior's appropriations bill an amendment to provide forty-two million dollars for the relocation of Centralia. After much political dickering, the bill was passed by 226 votes to 186.

Although not everyone in Centralia was pleased with the outcome of the vote, those who wanted to rid themselves of the constant threat of fire and gas now began life over in New Centralia, seven miles west of their former hometown.

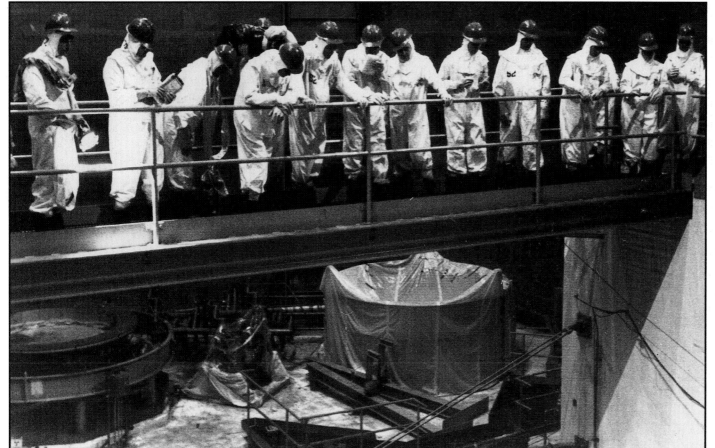

ABOVE: America's most famous industrial accident in recent history occurred at the Three Mile Island nuclear power plant near Harrisburg, Pennsylvania. On March 28, 1979, radioactive material leaked out of a containment building and radioactive fumes escaped into the atmosphere. People throughout the surrounding area were warned to stay indoors.

LEFT: Members of the President's Commission on Three Mile Island examining one of the two nuclear reactors at the Pennsylvania power plant in May 1979. The commission was investigating possible causes of the plant's leak.

ABOVE: A year and a half after the radioactive leak at the Three Mile Island nuclear power plant, Metropolitan Edison technicians prepare to enter the containment building for the third time since the unit was shut down.

BELOW: Within minutes of the leak in August 1985 at the Union Carbide plant in Institute, West Virginia, 135 people had been sickened by aldicarb oxime fumes. More than twenty people were admitted to hospitals complaining of eye and throat irritation, and vomiting. The leak was caused by three faulty gaskets in a storage tank.

RIGHT: A smaller, less deadly version of the gas leak in Bhopal, India, the leak at Union Carbide's Institute, West Virginia, pesticide plant passed aldicarb oxime into the atmosphere on August 11, 1985. The plant is shown before the disaster.

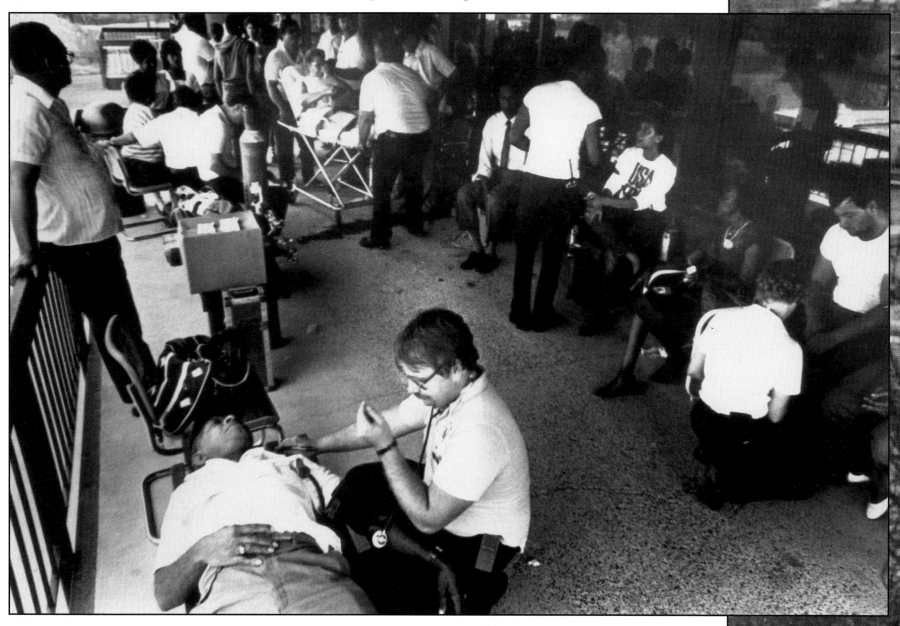

CHAPTER EIGHT

TRANSPORTATION DISASTERS

Most transportation disasters happen in a split second. The *Challenger*, for example, exploded in the air before its crew probably even knew what was happening. The *Eastland* steamer overturned in the Chicago River in an instant. Others take longer to claim their victims. The *Titanic*, for example, sank slowly for hours on end. Whatever the time it takes for a transportation system to go wrong, the results can be deadly.

LEFT: Salvage workers used pumps and derricks to raise the capsized steamer *Eastland* out of the Chicago River in July 1915.

RIGHT: On May 8, 1937, the Naval Board of Inquiry began investigating the *Hindenburg* fire and subsequent crash. Members of the Board are seen at the nose of the airship.

THE EASTLAND STEAMER, CHICAGO RIVER 1915

The weather was drizzly on July 24, 1915, but 7,500 pleasure seekers looked forward with excitement to their excursion from Chicago to Michigan City, Indiana. This annual event, sponsored by the Hawthorne Club, attracted thousands of people each year.

At about 6.00 a.m., passengers started boarding the *Eastland*, one of five steamer ships that would take them to the picnic. By 6.30 a.m., more than 2,500 people had packed themselves tightly onto the ship's decks.

The *Eastland* measured 265 feet long and was both narrow and tall. For five years after the ship was built, sailors complained of her tendency to list. To compensate for this tendency, the ship carried ballast tanks filled with water. The crew could alter the level in the water ballast tanks on either side to steady the ship.

Shortly before 7.00 a.m., the ship's engineer, Joseph M. Erickson, detected a list to port. The tilt was caused when many of the passengers on board scurried to the port side to be photographed by someone on shore. Erickson released water from one of the ballast tanks on the starboard side. For a moment, the ship righted, but then the swaying back and forth resumed. Immediately after the harbor master asked the *Eastland's* captain,

RIGHT: At 6:00 a.m. on July 24, 1915, passengers started boarding the steam excursion ship, *Eastland*, on the Chicago River for a sightseeing trip to Michigan City, Indiana. 2,500 people were tightly packed on board when the boat suddenly capsized. More than 800 people drowned in the accident. Here, rescue workers search for bodies.

BELOW: The *Eastland's* Captain, Harry Pederson (middle) was arrested after the disaster because he had interfered with rescue efforts. Later, criminal charges were brought against him by families of the victims.

RIGHT: Families of the victims of the *Eastland* disaster line up to enter the temporary morgue.

BELOW RIGHT: The bodies of the *Eastland* victims were set out in the Second Regiment Armory after the disaster.

BELOW: Survivors of the *Eastland* disaster making their way to shore from the *Kenosha*.

ABOVE: Rescue workers remove the bodies of victims of the *Eastland* disaster. Workers from a nearby warehouse tossed crates into the water for survivors to use as floats after they had pushed their way out of the sinking ship.

Harry Pedersen, if he was ready to pull away from the dock, the steamer listed sharply to port. Sixty crew members, knowing full well what lay ahead, leaped onto the dock. They reached safety before the steamer suddenly capsized. Floating on her port side, the *Eastland* took tons of water on board. Inside, thousands of passengers tried to fight their way out of the ship. Cries for help from the passengers mingled with shrieks of dispair from the onlookers.

Workers from a nearby warehouse tossed crates into the water for people to use as floats until they could reach the shore. Other workers started burning through the starboard side of the ship with a torch, trying to create a hole through which stranded passengers could climb. Captain Pedersen was furious. How dare these people cut a hole in his ship? Before the rescuers could resume their work, police had to arrest Pedersen to keep him out of the way.

Rescuers pulled the dead to the shore and took the bodies to the Second Regiment Armory. Of the 2,500 people on board, 812 had drowned in the whirling mass of water. Almost three quarters of the people killed were between fifteen and thirty years old.

THE HINDENBURG, LAKEHURST, NEW JERSEY 1937

The U.S. Navy was proud of its airships, or dirigibles, in the 1930s. They were huge, they were capable of carrying large numbers of men for deployment anywhere in the world, and they were the latest in transport systems.

The famous *Hindenburg* disaster was one that should rightly be characterized as both American and German. The *Hindenburg* was the pride of Nazi Germany but, when tragedy struck, the dirigible carried among its passengers several American citizens.

At 804 feet long, the *Hindenburg* was the largest dirigible ever constructed. Its quarters could comfortably accommodate ninety-seven passengers and a crew of sixty-one. It could hold enough fuel to fly 8,000 miles, and was filled with seven million cubic feet of hydrogen. Hydrogen is the lightest known gas, but it is

not only extremely flammable, but also explosive. Other dirigibles of the day achieved their height by using helium, a much safer gas than hydrogen, if not as light.

In 1936 the *Hindenburg* made ten transatlantic flights. In May 1937, the airship was again headed across the ocean at eighty-four miles an hour for the seventy-six hour trip to Lakehurst, New Jersey. On this trip the ship carried a crew of sixty-one and thirty-six passengers, who had each paid 400 dollars for the privilege of crossing the Atlantic in the world's finest airship.

BELOW: Department of Commerce inspectors examining the forward port motor of the *Hindenburg* on May 20, 1937. Dr. Hugo Eckener, an expert in airship technology, testified that a small spark from a thunder squall had ignited hydrogen leaking from the rear of the airship. Others speculated that sabotage was the real cause.

RIGHT: The German dirigible, the *Hindenburg,* was approaching the landing station at Lakehurst, New Jersey, when she suddenly burst into flames. Filled with seven million cubic feet of hydrogen, the *Hindenburg* was carrying 97 people – 61 crew members and 36 passengers – on the day of the disaster, May 6, 1937.

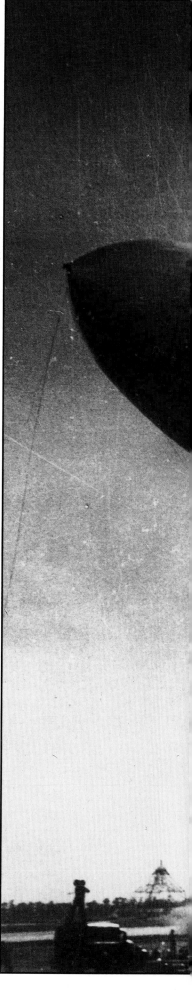

The interior of the *Hindenburg* was luxurious. It boasted a large dining room where all the passengers could take their meals together. Tables in the dining room were adorned with fine linen and fresh flowers. In the lounge, passengers could play a grand piano covered in yellow pigskin. From the promenade decks with Plexiglas windows, passengers often spent hours gazing down at the landscape or seascape 800 feet below them. The walls of the smoking room were covered in yellow pigskin, and it was only here that passengers were allowed to smoke.

Originally the *Hindenburg* was scheduled to land at 5.00 a.m., but bad weather caused a delay, and the rescheduled docking time was for sunset. There was then a further delay when a rainstorm blew into the area at about 3.00 p.m. that afternoon. Around 6.00 p.m., the *Hindenburg* was finally ready to dock, and the ground crew prepared to catch the lines that would drop from the dirigible for tying. At the scene were a thousand spectators who exchanged waves with the *Hindenburg's* passengers standing at the open windows. At 7.23 p.m., the ropes dropped from the ship.

The first person on the ground to notice something awry was Chief Boatswain's Mate R. H. Ward. He noticed that the fabric covering of the ship was fluttering near its tail. Gas was escaping from the rear of the ship. The ship's captain, Max Pruss, realized that the airship was approaching the docking tower too fast, so he ordered the crew to reverse the two rear engines. Suddenly sparks shot out of the exhaust.

A gigantic explosion occurred as the sparks turned the escaping gas into flames. On board, some of the passengers were hurled from the exploding dirigible, and fell to the ground. Some of the crew members, knowing that the guide lines had already been lowered in preparation for docking, jumped toward the lines. Those who missed their target plunged to the ground.

The *Hindenburg* continued to explode as the flames raced from one compartment of gas to the next. The airship broke into two parts almost instantly. First the tail dropped to the ground, then the nose crashed into a flaming pile on the ground. Some members of the ground crew were injured as pieces of flaming fabric dropped from the air. The heat given off from the flaming mass was intense.

As the flames licked toward the passenger compartments, one mother on board picked up her three children, one by one, and threw them out the window. Only she and one child survived the jump. Some passengers watched helplessly as their families were consumed by flames. Others walked from the inferno in dazed concentration, as their clothes sizzled on their backs. Miraculously, all but thirty-six of the ninety-seven people on board the airship survived.

Dr. Hugo Eckener, an expert in dirigible technology, examined the wreckage during the weeks following the explosion and conducted interviews with the surviving passengers and the ground crew. His theory, which was accepted as the final word, was that a spark from a thunderstorm had ignited the gas at the rear of ship.

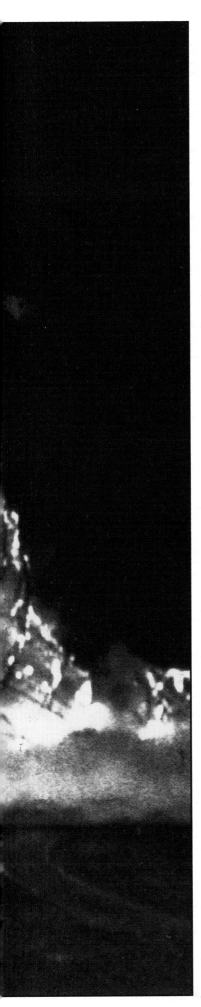

LEFT: At first the blazing *Hindenburg* seemed to hang in the sky, then she suddenly crashed to the ground, where flames reduced the airship to a skeleton.

RIGHT: Captain Max Pruss, commander of the *Hindenburg*, was severely burned in the disaster. On May 7, 1937, he was transferred from a hospital in Lakewood, New Jersey, to Cornell Medical Center in New York, where he recovered from his injuries.

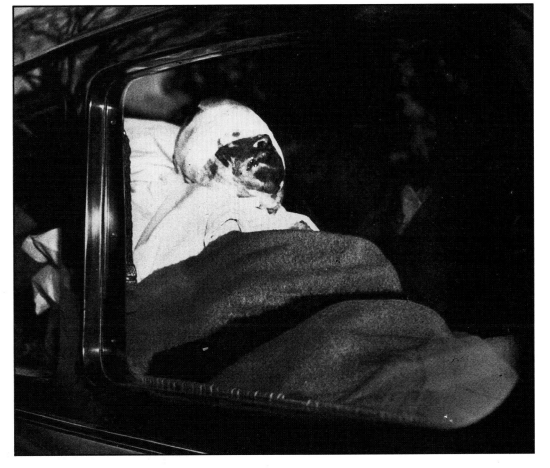

Others suggested sabotage as the cause of the explosion. The *Hindenburg* was a symbol of Nazi Germany, and many of the crew members belonged to the party. Some people assumed that the fire was started deliberately to destroy the dirigible of which Adolph Hitler was so proud.

After the disaster, President Franklin D. Roosevelt began negotiations with Germany to develop a plan by which Germany could purchase helium. America had a monopoly on helium, which was produced from natural gas. Helium's advantage over hydrogen is that it is nonflammable.

Among the spectators that evening was Herbert Morrison, a radio announcer from station WLS in Chicago. His words, broadcast that night, have become inseparable from the tragedy: "Here it comes, ladies and gentlemen. And what a sight it is, a thrilling one, a marvelous sight… oh, oh, oh!…. It's burst into flames… oh this is terrible, oh my, …It is burning, bursting into flames and is falling… oh!… This is one of the worst… oh! It's a terrific sight… oh!… and all the humanity!"

RIGHT: A group of inspectors from the Department of Commerce began their own investigation of the *Hindenburg* disaster on May 10, 1937.

BELOW: Thirty-six of the ninety-seven people on board the *Hindenburg* perished in the fire. Some jumped to their deaths from the flaming blimp; others stayed on board and were consumed by the blaze. Rescue teams worked all night removing the bodies.

The Akron 1933

On Tuesday, April 4, 1933, the U.S. Navy's great airship, the *Akron*, crashed into the sea during severe thunderstorms.

The *Akron* and its crew of seventy-six left Lakehurst, New Jersey, at 7.30 p.m. on April 4. The ship's mission was to fly along the New England coast to calibrate radio stations. Throughout the flight the crew was forced to keep changing course due to storms. At about 12.30 a.m. that night, the ship started to toss about in the turbulent skies. Suddenly the ship lurched, and the control wires to the upper rudder snapped. Lieutenant Commander Herbert V. Wiley tried to steer the ship with the remaining rudder, but moments later the control wires to that also broke. Suddenly the ship began to fall. At 300 feet above the sea, Commander Wiley gave the order: "Stand by for crash." Thirty seconds later the airship crashed into the sea, and violent waves wrecked the craft. Some men were able to swim away from the wreckage. Others sank along with it.

Nearby, the German oil tanker *Phoebus* was heading toward the American shores. The tanker's crew spotted the wrecked *Akron* and began searching for survivors. Four members of the *Akron's* crew were pulled from the stormy waters; only three lived to tell their story. All through the early morning hours, the *Phoebus* searched for crewmen in the dark waters of the Atlantic.

At about 10.45 a.m. on April 5, the Navy dispatched another blimp, the J-3, to search for the *Akron's* crew. This, too, fell prey to the storm, and two of its seven-man crew were lost.

RIGHT: The wreckage of the U.S. Navy's airship, the *Akron,* is hauled out of the ocean by the U.S.S. *Falcon.* The *Akron* crashed into the Atlantic Ocean on April 4, 1933, during a severe thunderstorm. Only three men of the seventy-six-member crew survived the crash.

THE DC-10 CRASH, CHICAGO 1979

On the afternoon of May 25, 1979, burning debris littered the grounds of a small abandoned airport in Chicago. Among the debris lay the dead – 272 people who had boarded American Flight 191 bound for Los Angeles.

The DC-10, manufactured by the McDonnell Douglas Corporation, was in trouble immediately after takeoff. An air traffic controller at Chicago's O'Hare Airport radioed to the pilot, "Do you want to come back?" There was no reply and, moments later, the personnel in the control tower saw the plane veer to the left and an engine drop off. Another eyewitness saw smoke coming from the plane's left wing engine immediately after takeoff.

Hours after the crash, the debris was still too hot for rescuers to search for bodies. However, by late afternoon, the bodies had been removed to a temporary morgue in a nearby hangar.

Residents in Chicago were fortunate in that the plane avoided hitting a gasoline storage tank belonging to the Standard Oil Company and crashed in one of the city's few open, unpopulated areas – an abandoned airfield. However, nearby mobile homes were hit by flaming debris, and two people at work near the crash site were fatally injured. One suffered burns over fifty percent of his body.

During investigations into the crash, inspectors found a nut and bolt, of the variety used to attach engine mounts to the underside of the wing, near the landing gate from which the DC-10 had departed. In addition, inspectors were puzzled as to why the pilot could not have flown the plane successfully on the two remaining engines. Had the wing structure been damaged when the engine and its mount fell off? Throughout the country, airlines grounded their DC-10s for thirty-eight days following the crash, only to resume operations, with more frequent inspections of the engine mounts.

The National Transportation Safety Board reported in December 1979 that the crash was caused by poor maintenance and the plane's structural design. The board called for stricter procedures in certifying new planes and for better monitoring of production and airline operations.

BELOW: Firemen searching for survivors in the wreckage of the American Airlines DC-10 that crashed near Chicago's O'Hare Airport. Flight 191 took off from O'Hare Airport on May 25, 1979. Moments later the left engine dropped off the plane, which then crashed onto the site of an old airfield just over a mile north of the airport, killing more than 270 people.

THE CHALLENGER 1986

"We have a report from the flight dynamics officer that the vehicle has exploded." These words by the Public Affairs Officer of NASA marked the end of the space shuttle *Challenger's* seventy-four-second flight, which resulted in the deaths of its seven-member crew.

More than a thousand spectators watched with wonder as the spacecraft lifted off its pad at 11.38 a.m. on January 28, 1986. As the craft turned into a fiery orange ball, the expressions on the spectators' faces slowly changed to horror.

The crew consisted of mission commander Francis R. Scobee, pilot Michael J. Smith, Judith A. Resnik, Ronald E. McNair, Ellison S. Onizuka, Gregory B. Jarvis, and Christa McAuliffe, a high-school teacher from Concord, New Hampshire. McAuliffe was the first civilian to take part in the U.S. space program. Her husband, two children, parents, friends, and students from Concord were among the spectators at Cape Canaveral that day.

The flight on January 28 was the shuttle's tenth mission. After liftoff, the craft sped ten miles up into the sky, reaching a speed of 1,977 miles per hour, then burst into flames.

Coast Guard ships were delayed about an hour before starting their search in the Atlantic Ocean for survivors and pieces of the *Challenger* because burning debris continued to fall from the sky. In addition, a huge toxic cloud formed when the fuel tanks, carrying 385,000 gallons of liquid hydrogen and 140,000 gallons of liquid oxygen, exploded, which meant that any rescuers entering the area would be endangering themselves. As the Coast Guard waited to search the sea, some debris washed ashore.

Immediately after the disaster, the worst in the history of the U.S. space program, officials speculated that the explosion had been caused by a leak either in the shuttle's hydrogen fuel tank or in the pipe that carried the fuel to the engines. If hydogen had come into contact with the oxygen in a separate fuel tank, an explosion would definitely have occurred.

Two days after the crash, officials reported that the solid-fuel booster rocket suddenly lost power ten seconds before the explosion. Flames that shot out of the booster burned through the external fuel tank to the liquid oxygen line inside. A few months later, NASA officials testified before a presidential investigating commission that a joint on the solid-fuel booster rocket

BELOW: The seven-member crew of the *Challenger* space shuttle. Left to right, back row: El Onizuka; Christa McAuliffe, a high-shool teacher from Concord, New Hampshire, and the first civilian to participate in the U.S. space program; Greg Jarvis; and Judy Resnik. Left to right, front row: Mike Smith; Dick Scobee, commander; and Ron McNair.

RIGHT: An employee at the Kennedy Space Center watches from the ground, as the *Challenger* explodes, with the loss of its seven-member crew.

had failed, causing the fuel tanks to explode.

On January 31, President and Mrs. Ronald Reagan attended a memorial service for the astronauts killed in the explosion. Grieving with the families and friends of the astronauts, President Reagan said, "Sometimes when we reach for the stars, we fall short."

The tragedy inspired many Americans to think "not again," as they recalled another space disaster nineteen years and one day before. On January 27, 1967, astronauts Virgil I. Grissom, Edward H. White, and Roger B. Chaffee climbed aboard the Apollo I spacecraft for a simulation of a flight to the moon that was to take place on February 21. After they had been inside the capsule for five hours, one of the astronauts suddenly blurted out: "Fire in the capsule." Fifteen seconds later, all three were dead. Although the precise cause of the fire was never determined, some people believe that a spark ignited the pure oxygen inside the capsule.

LEFT: An overall view of the *Challenger's* path from the launching pad to the site of the explosion.

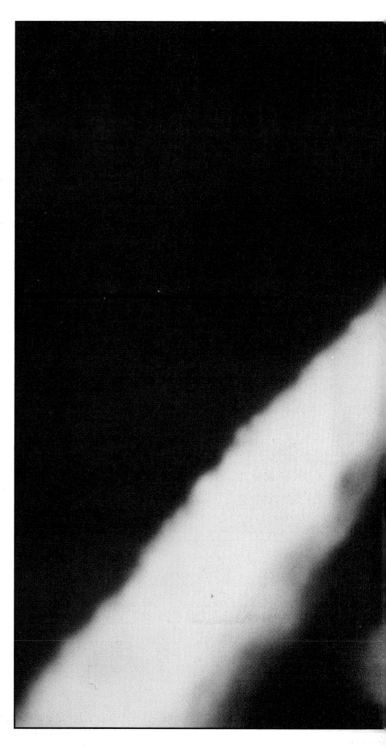

BELOW: At 73.201 seconds into the flight, there was a flash between the *Challenger* and one of the fuel tanks.

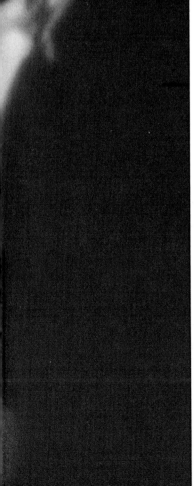

ABOVE: A close-up view of the *Challenger* explosion taken with a 70mm tracking camera.

RIGHT: As the wreckage from the *Challenger* space shuttle was pulled from the Atlantic Ocean, it was stored in a tent at the Kennedy Space Center for investigation. Ultimately, inspectors determined the cause of the *Challenger* explosion to be the failure of a joint on the solid-fuel booster rocket.

LEFT: On January 27, 1967, astronauts Virgil I. (Gus) Grissom, Edward H. White, and Roger B. Chaffee entered the *Apollo I* space capsule for a moon flight simulation. After only five hours in the capsule, the three astronauts died in a flash fire.

BELOW: Technicians examining the exterior of the *Apollo I* spacecraft after the January 27, 1967, disaster.

ABOVE: Components of the *Apollo I* spacecraft were organized in a storage area for examination. The exact cause of the flash fire was never determined, but experts speculated that a spark had ignited the pure oxygen inside the capsule.

BELOW: The burned interior of the *Apollo I* spacecraft as viewed through the hatch.

TRIPLE SCREW STEAMER "TITANIC" WAS THE LARGEST AND FINEST VESSEL IN THE WORLD: 882½ FEET LONG, 45,000 TONS REGISTER, 92½ FEET WIDE

ABOVE: The British White Star Line, the *Titanic,* was a luxury liner capable of carrying more than 2,200 passengers and crew. On the fifth day of her maiden voyage, from Southampton to New York, the *Titanic* sank, after hitting an iceberg on April 14, 1912.

RIGHT: A re-enactment of the receipt of the *Titanic*'s distress signal by a radio operator on the *Carpathia,* the first rescue ship on the scene, where 711 survivors, mostly women and children, were packed into lifeboats.

RIGHT: The April 16, 1912 edition of *The New York Times* covered the *Titanic* disaster. The newspaper's estimate of 1,250 deaths was too low; 1,517 people died, some because of an inadequate supply of lifeboats. Among the dead were Isidor Straus, a New York millionaire, and Colonel John Jacob Astor, great-grandson of the fur trader and financier by the same name.

BELOW: The world was shocked by the sinking of the *Titanic*. Here, English Boy Scouts collect funds for the families of victims.

The New York Times.

"All the News That's Fit to Print."

NEW YORK, TUESDAY, APRIL 16, 1912 — TWENTY-FOUR PAGES.

ONE CENT

THE WEATHER.

TITANIC SINKS FOUR HOURS AFTER HITTING ICEBERG; 866 RESCUED BY CARPATHIA, PROBABLY 1250 PERISH; ISMAY SAFE, MRS. ASTOR MAYBE, NOTED NAMES MISSING

Col. Astor and Bride, Isidor Straus and Wife, and Maj. Butt Aboard.

"RULE OF SEA" FOLLOWED

Women and Children Put Over in Lifeboats and Are Supposed to be Safe on Carpathia.

PICKED UP AFTER 8 HOURS

Vincent Astor Calls at White Star Office for News of His Father and Leaves Weeping.

FRANKLIN HOPEFUL ALL DAY

Manager of the Line Insisted Titanic Was Unsinkable Even After She Had Gone Down.

HEAD OF THE LINE ABOARD

J. Bruce Ismay Making First Trip to Gigantic Ship That Was to Surpass All Others.

Biggest Liner Plunges to the Bottom at 2:20 A.M.

RESCUERS THERE TOO LATE

Except to Pick Up the Few Hundreds Who Took to the Lifeboats.

WOMEN AND CHILDREN FIRST

Cunarder Carpathia Rushing to New York with the Survivors.

SEA SEARCH FOR OTHERS

The California Stands By on Chance of Picking Up Other Boats or Rafts.

OLYMPIC SENDS THE NEWS

Only Ship to Flash Wireless Messages to Shore After the Disaster.

The Lost Titanic Being Towed Out of Belfast Harbor.

CAPT. E. J. SMITH, Commander of the Titanic.

PARTIAL LIST OF THE SAVED.

Includes Bruce Ismay, Mrs. Widener, Mrs. H. B. Harris, and an incomplete name, suggesting Mrs. Astor's.

CAPE RACE, N. F., Tuesday, April 16.—Following is a partial list of survivors among the first-class passengers of the Titanic, received by the Marconi wireless station this morning from the Carpathia, via the steamship Olympic.

ABOVE: Air Florida Flight 90 took off from Washington National Airport on January 13, 1982, and almost immediately crashed into the 14th Street Bridge over the Potomac River. Seventy-four people on board the plane died in the crash, as did four people in cars on the bridge at the time of the crash.

RIGHT: Salvage operations continued for several days after the crash of Air Florida Flight 90. National Transportation Safety Board inspectors examine the wreckage. The cause of the crash was determined to be ice on the wings.

RIGHT: Rescue workers lifting a section of the Air Florida plane out of the Potomac River, a week after the plane crashed into the 14th Street Bridge in Washington, D.C.

RIGHT: In freezing temperatures, a rescue worker searches for survivors amid the wreckage of the Amtrak train. Ten days later, investigators announced that the men operating the Conrail locomotives were responsible for the accident.

BELOW: Rescue workers recover the body of a victim of the worst disaster in Amtrak's history, which occurred on January 4, 1987. A passenger train was derailed after being struck by three Conrail engines near Baltimore, Maryland. Fifteen people died in the accident.